Doctrines in Genesis

Doctrines in Genesis

Foundational Truths from the First Book of the Bible

by

J.R. Dickens

Doctrines in Genesis:
Foundational Truths from the First Book of the Bible

Scripture quoted by permission.

For quotations designated (NKJV): Scripture taken from the New King James Version. Copyright © 1979, 1980, 1982 by Thomas Nelson, Inc. Used by permission. All rights reserved.

For quotations designated (ESV): Scripture quotations are from The Holy Bible, English Standard Version®, copyright © 2001 by Crossway Bibles, a division of Good News Publishers. Used by permission. All rights reserved.

Cover design by J.R. Dickens using Kindle Direct Publishing graphics and templates.

Author's cover photo copyright © J.R. Dickens.

ISBN (paperback): 978-0-9992870-3-3

Copyright © 2023 by J.R. Dickens.
All Rights Reserved.

Printed in the United States of America.

Table of Contents

Table of Contents 1

Acknowledgements 5

Introduction 6

Session 1: Truth and Reason 8

    Scripture (Acts 26:24-27) 8

    Introduction 8

    The Madness of Relativism (Vain Idols) 10

    Why Genesis? 16

    How Do We Know Anything? 18

    The Necessity of Revelation 20

    Antithesis and Dichotomy from the First Verse 23

    The Source of All Confusion 24

    Scripture Plus Skepticism Equals Liberalism (Mystical "God Words") 27

    Only Two Destinations 30

Session 2: The God Who Is 34

    Scripture (Gen 1:1-3) 34

    Introduction 34

    The Pre-Existence of God 37

    The Power of God 44

    The Purpose of God 50

The Personality of God 52

The Promises of God 55

The Confrontation on Mars Hill 57

Session 3: Creation from Nothing 61

Scripture (Gen 1:1-25) 61

Introduction 63

No One Was There 70

Why Creation? Because of What it Reveals About God 73

Science and Scripture 76

No Common Ground 77

The Idol of Wood 79

Man on the Escalator 82

A Miracle by any Definition 83

Inconvenient Scientific Facts, and the Fallacy of Consensus 84

Session 4: Man Made in God's Image 90

Scripture (Gen 1:26-28) 90

Introduction 90

Science Says: We are the Sum of Our Parts 94

Humanism Says: We are Bodies Without Souls 95

Economics Says: You're Worth What You Produce 98

Incomparable Worth 101

Imago Dei: The Breath of Life 105

One Man Adam, One Human Race 109

    Bringing Life from the Dust 110

Session 5: Creation Ruined 116

    Scripture (Gen 3:1-7) 116

    Introduction 116

    "Man is Great, But he is Cruel" 121

    From Perfection to Ruin 122

    No Small Failure 124

    Trust or Doubt 126

    The Bad News About Man's Condition 127

    From Eden to Utopia 130

    Spiritual Warfare 132

    The Enemy's Tactics 134

    How Bad is Bad? 135

    "Who Then Can Be Saved?" 141

Session 6: Redemption and Restoration 144

    Scripture (Gen 3:8-21) 144

    Introduction 145

    The High Price of a Soul 148

    Not by the Works of the Law 149

    . . . But by the Works of Another 151

    The Skins of the Elder Brother 152

    Where Justice and Mercy Meet 156

    The Wages of Sin . . . and the Gift of Grace 157

Recap: Hard Questions—*Answered* 159

About J.R. Dickens 163

Acknowledgements

I would like to express my thanks to Covenant Presbyterian Church (PCA) in Lufkin, Texas: Pastor Mark O'Neill, along with elders Bill Craig, Kirk Fearing, and Cecil Paul Mott.

Many others from this church played a role in the preparation and presentation of the conference. Their help is greatly appreciated.

Introduction

The material in this book is transcribed from the lectures delivered as a Reformation conference for Covenant Presbyterian Church (PCA), Lufkin, Texas, on October 30, 2021. The recordings of this conference can be found on SermonAudio, either on the church's page or the author's page.

The subject is daunting and this book represents little more than an introduction. We can infer a long list of essential doctrines of the Christian faith in the book of Genesis. In these lectures, we will address the following:

- truth and reason; thesis and antithesis
- the existence of God
- six-day creation / young earth
- anthropology: man made in God's image; man made male and female
- the Fall of man and the Curse
- redemption and restoration

Additional doctrines include:

- marriage and family
- authority structures
- Sabbath observance
- speech and language

- languages and nations
- law and ethics
- dominion and stewardship
- vocation and division of labor
- revelation
- personal responsibility
- regulated worship
- ceremonial law
- priesthood and mediation
- angels and demons
- spiritual warfare
- covenantal theology
- eschatology
- temporal judgment
- geological catastrophism
- death, burial, and resurrection

From this list we can see that defending the Christian faith means defending the book of Genesis as our starting point.

Since the material in this book is transcribed from the six recorded lectures, it has been edited only slightly in order to correct a few errors and smooth out a few bumps. For better or for worse, it reflects my run-on style of extemporaneous speaking. I trust that the reader will find it engaging and edifying in spite of its grammatical challenges.

Scripture footnotes indicate the Bible translation when directly quoted. Paraphrased fragments are not cited.

Session 1: Truth and Reason

Scripture (Acts 26:24-27)

> Now as he thus made his defense, Festus said with a loud voice, "Paul, you are beside yourself! Much learning is driving you mad!" But he said, "I am not mad, most noble Festus, but speak the words of truth and reason. For the king, before whom I also speak freely, knows these things; for I am convinced that none of these things escapes his attention, since this thing was not done in a corner. King Agrippa, do you believe the prophets? I know that you do believe."[1]

Introduction

Thank you for that introduction, and good morning to everyone. It's not a small thing to ask you to give up part or even all of your Saturday to come out and listen to someone talk, but I appreciate your willingness to do that, and I am grateful to be here with you today.

I'm going to start by telling a little story on Pastor Mark. I'm sure he won't mind *too* much. We'll see. He'll let me know afterwards. It was the summer of 2009 and we were just coming to the close of a certain study, and I think it was an Old Testament study. It may have been Trey O'Rear who was leading that particular study, and Mark

---

[1] Acts 26:24-27 (NKJV).

approached me and said, "Is there a book of the Old Testament you'd like to teach next for the Sunday school?" And of course my mind's already going around about this and I said, "Yes—the book of Genesis." I'm not sure what his response was going to be, but it was kind of a curious response. He said, "So are you thinking the first 11 chapters or so?" And at this point, I'm having to have a little conversation with myself and say, *if I tell him I want to teach the whole thing, he's going to say, no, that's going to take too long, we're not going to do that.* So I equivocated my response and said, "Why don't we just get started and see how it goes?" And we got started that summer, 2009, and we brought our study of Genesis to a conclusion in December of 2010. As best I can reckon, it took about 15 months. There were about 60 lessons, but frankly, I lost count. There are 50 chapters in Genesis, of course. And even with the goal of teaching one chapter each week—which is really inadequate for probably any book of the Bible—it still took the better part of a year and a half to get through that study. And it was a delightful time. In my own experience of it, it reminded me of a scene from the *Chronicles of Narnia: The Voyage of the Dawn Treader*, where the kids are in the room and they're looking at the picture of the *Dawn Treader* on the wall, and then all of a sudden they can smell the sea spray, and then they can feel it, and then suddenly they're in the picture. And it was a lot like that, just being pulled into the narrative of the life of these men, these patriarchs, men of God, but obviously fallen. And it was just a delightful time for all of us.

So in a sense, it feels like being back here. And you know, the older you get, the passage of time, you lose track of it. It's like when I saw Mark and Bill this morning, and it's like, "Hi," and I'm thinking, *wait a minute, I haven't seen them in a year and a half. I should probably do more than wave.* So it literally has been more than 10 years since we finished that study. And yet, this morning, it feels a little like picking up where we left off.

The Madness of Relativism (Vain Idols)

I've continued to think about the book of Genesis over the years, and the importance of it. And even though it's the case that we tend to focus the controversy in Genesis over the question of *creation*, when you take a step back from it, you realize, *wait a minute, Genesis contains virtually all the important doctrines of the Christian faith.* It's not just a question of how did God create, but it's a question of where do we get our most fundamental Christian doctrines? And so the defense of Genesis, and the teaching of it, is an important aspect of our Christian lives, and we should not neglect it.

So as we think about this first session, I've titled it *Truth and Reason*. I might add to that, *Truth and Reason in an Age of Madness*. And by the way, there was a scripture reading that goes along with this. So, let me turn your attention, as we start this session, to the book of Acts in chapter 26.

You may not believe me when I say this, but I selected the title for this session before I found this passage in the book of Acts. It's actually the *New King James Version* that says it just the way that I want to, so I'm going to read from the *New King James*. But in this passage in Acts, starting in verse 24, Paul has just appealed his case to Caesar through Festus, and then King Agrippa comes through town, and King Agrippa wants to hear Paul for himself, so the royal court is convened and Paul is brought in and he begins a long defense. We're not going to read the whole defense of Paul in this section, but I'm going to pick it up at that point where it hits home in verse 24 of Acts 26.

> Now as he thus made his defense, Festus said with a loud voice, "Paul, you are beside yourself! Much learning is driving you mad!" But he said, "*I am not mad, most noble Festus, but speak the words of truth and reason.* For the king, before whom I also speak freely, knows these things; for I am convinced that none of these things escapes his attention, since this thing was not done in a corner. King Agrippa, do you believe the prophets? I know that you do believe."[2]

Now what strikes me about this passage—and the idea that we're going to pick up on—look at what Paul says. It starts with the *denial*. What's

---

[2] Acts 26:24-27 (NKJV).

the denial? *I am not mad but I speak the words of truth and reason.* And frankly it's either one or the other. You either have words of truth and reason or you have madness, and this contrast shows up many times throughout scripture. We think in terms of psychological disease. We try to find human or biological explanations for that—behavioral explanations—those kinds of things—but the connection in scripture is that when you begin to abandon truth and reason, you literally go mad. You go insane. You no longer have a grasp on truth and you no longer have the ability to think clearly or properly. And isn't that where we are in our culture today?

If you think—and you might think this, I certainly do—I look around and I think, *am I the only one who's still sane?* Because everything I see around me seems like madness and chaos. I'm listening to what's being said, I'm listening to what's being spoken as if it were true, and yet the narrative is so contradictory and so confusing that you can't make sense out of it. And that's the madness of our times. When we begin to disconnect ourselves from the truth, we literally have no foundation.

Now, I want to make a connection for you. And to do that, first, I'm going to turn to a small book in the back of the Old Testament, the book of Habakkuk. And I'm going to look at a couple of verses from the end of chapter two—verses 18 to 20 in the book of Habakkuk. It's among the Minor Prophets. It's the fifth book from the end of the Old Testament.

So, chapter 2, verses 18 to 20, where he says:

> "What profit is an idol
>   when its maker has shaped it,
>   a metal image, *a teacher of lies?*
> For its maker trusts in his own creation
>   when he makes speechless idols!
> Woe to him who says to a wooden thing, Awake;
>   to a silent stone, Arise!
> Can this teach?
> Behold, it is overlaid with gold and silver,
>   and there is no breath at all in it.
> But the LORD is in his holy temple;
>   let all the earth keep silence before him."[3]

And I want to pick up on the idea in that particular passage about this thing that has *no speech* and yet it's *a teacher of lies*. And another passage that I want to turn your attention to, which is probably a little easier to find and a bit more familiar, is in Psalm 115.

I'll start at the beginning of Psalm 115 and read down through verse 8.

> Not to us, O LORD, not to us, but to your name give glory,
>   for the sake of your steadfast love and your faithfulness!

---
[3] Hab 2:18-20 (ESV).

> Why should the nations say,
> > "Where is their God?"
> Our God is in the heavens;
> > he does all that he pleases.
> Their idols are silver and gold,
> > the work of human hands. . . .

And this is the part I want you to consider very carefully this morning:

> They have mouths, but do not speak;
> > eyes, but do not see.
> They have ears, but do not hear;
> > noses, but do not smell.
> They have hands, but do not feel;
> > feet, but do not walk;
> > and they do not make a sound in their throat. . . .

And here's the clincher:

> *Those who make them become like them;*
> > *so do all who trust in them.*[4]

So let that passage ring in your mind a moment. What do we become when we start making idols for ourselves? Speechless. Blind. Deaf. Unable to see or perceive anything. Unable to speak. Powerless. It's a profound statement—that when we begin making idols for ourselves,

---

[4] Ps 115:1-8 (ESV).

we become like the thing that we make. And over and over again—and it's often the case that in scripture when the Lord is talking about idols, he's doing it in kind of a mocking way. *You make your idol and you prop it up. If you don't prop it up, it's going to fall over because it can't even hold itself up. You have to carry it from one side of the room to the other*, and so forth, *because it cannot move under its own power. Or, you carve an idol out of wood and then with the rest of the wood, you build yourself a fire to warm yourself.* Those kinds of things.

The folly of idolatry shows up over and over again and it's one of our chief sins—and we are certainly not immune to it in our own day. But this is what we might call the madness of relativism.

Now what is the creed of relativism? *There is no such thing as absolute truth.* And we notice that statement is constructed in a logical fashion, and that it's a contradiction. And so if we start with a contradiction, then that means we have already abandoned *reason* at the outset. And so we have this idea that there's no such thing as *truth*, and in order for us to declare that there's no such thing as truth, we first have to abandon *reason* in order to even make the statement. And so you see the madness that we are left with in that scenario.

Why Genesis?

So we take a minute at the beginning of this conference to think about the question, *why the book of Genesis—why is it important?* There are those, unfortunately, who think that the Old Testament is of very little importance to the Christian. Some will even say *there's nothing there for you*. And yet that's a very foolish thing to say, because I seem to recall Jesus taking a walk with a couple of disciples after the resurrection and saying to them, *starting with Moses and the prophets, opening the scriptures to show to them all that the scriptures say concerning him*. And where does the book of Moses start, or the work of Moses? Well, Genesis is actually called *the first book of Moses*. Genesis is a title that was added later on, after the Septuagint.[5]

So Genesis, if we think about what Genesis is teaching us in just these first three chapters, the first two chapters concern creation, the third chapter concerns the Fall and the Curse that follows. Just within those first three chapters we could pretty much address all the crazy kinds of issues that we're facing today. And that's what we'll see as we go through the course of the day.

---

[5] The Greek translation of the Old Testament, dated around 250 B.C.

Now in terms of doctrines—if we start looking at Genesis in terms of doctrines—we're going to find dozens of Christian doctrines in the book of Genesis. I was originally hoping I could get nine sessions this weekend, and thinking *nine will get us started*, but the elders decided that six was probably about all we could do at once. So I squeezed it down. But trying to teach something about the doctrines in Genesis in just a few sessions is a hard thing to do because there are so many things that we could choose, so many doctrines.

Now, Genesis is an *historical* book. It's not a doctrinal book. We think of doctrinal books—Romans is one of our favorites as Reformed Presbyterians. The book of Hebrews is also a great theological book. But Genesis is history, and yet within that history, we see the unfolding of God's work and God's plans; God's relationship with man and how he deals with man; the Fall and how he's going to begin to deal with the Fall. That Genesis, from beginning to end, has been described as the narrative of redemption—that it's God's unfolding story of how he relates to mankind, especially after the Fall. And of course, that culminates in the person and the work of Christ, who is the answer to everything that was lost in that Fall of Genesis 3.

How Do We Know Anything?

Now, as we come to this, we have an important question to ask. And this is where I'm going to get a little philosophical and a little nerdy for a minute and throw out a big word called *epistemology*. Epistemology is the science of knowledge—it helps us answer the question of how we know what we know. We might ask the question more fundamentally and say *how do we know anything?* That's a profoundly important question—the kind of question philosophers have been wrestling with for literally thousands of years. And if we're going to know something, we have to have some kind of a starting point, and that's the challenge.

Well, I did a little word study on *epistemology*. I look at this word, and I think, *that looks Greek*. So I started digging around in the Greek lexicon. And so it's a compound word. You might notice the *epi-* on the front is a prefix. And so we need to know, what does the prefix mean? How does it modify the root? And what is the root of this thing? And so you dig down a couple of layers from *epistemos* to *ephistemos* to *stao*, which refers to *standing*. Okay. And then what does the *epi-* do to that? And it means *to stand upon*. And that's an interesting little word study because it gives us the idea that we need something to stand on. And that's what we're looking for—we need truth. We need a standard for truth, and of course it's going to drive us to the word of God.

We need to spend some time thinking about how do we know anything, because think about how we learn anything. Well, first of all, we need *language*, for example, or we need *senses*. And then when it comes to revelation, we need to be able to use our *minds*. We need to be able to use *logic*. We might even notice there are different kinds of letters that are combined in different kinds of ways that mean different kinds of things. And when we combine those words in certain ways into sentences following grammatical rules, they have meaning. So we need that kind of thing as a starting point.

It seems to me that epistemology is a bit of a circular argument, no matter what your view is. So we have to *assume* something in order to *learn* something. And then we need some kind of process to help us work through what's true and what's not true. And that's where logic comes into play. And one of the most important laws of logic that come into play is *the law of non-contradiction*—meaning that an idea and its opposite can't both be true at the same time and in the same relationship. And then that leads us to an idea that we call *antithesis*—that if something is true and something else says the opposite, they can't both be true at the same time. And that opposites are distinct. We can make *distinctions*.

The Necessity of Revelation

One of the unfortunate consequences of some of the more modern philosophy—thinking of Hegel and his dialectical synthesis—is the idea, yeah, we have thesis and we have antithesis, but we're going to mush them together and call it synthesis. Well, suddenly, we can't make any distinctions at all, and that becomes a real problem when it comes to understanding what is true and what is false. How can we determine the difference between right and wrong in a system like that? And the answer is that we can't, and maybe that's the point. So that brings me to the next point which is the necessity of revelation.

Now scripture describes revelation in two different ways. We talk about *natural* revelation—which is God making himself visible through the things that are created—and we also have revelation through *scripture*. Now, at different times and different places—as it says at the opening of Hebrews—God revealed himself in different ways, but in these latter days he has revealed himself through his Son, and specifically through the written word—the written accounts of the life and the work of Christ. So we, in our age, have the word of God that is complete from beginning to end. And it's important to have in mind that this book is our standard. We're going to see, for example, when we look at what happened in the Fall, God makes Adam and Eve, he places them in the

Garden, and then he gives them a commandment. In other words, he gives them a *word*. And he says, *of all the trees in the Garden you may freely eat, but of the one that's in the midst of the Garden you may not eat of it, for in the day you eat of it you shall surely die.* There's the truth standard, the measuring stick. And then a Serpent comes along and says, *did God really say that? Is that what he said? Is that what he meant? No, he didn't mean that. You're not going to die.* So suddenly we see the first dilemma. We see the first challenge to truth. And if we abandon that standard of truth as Adam and Eve did in that moment, then we're almost certain to fall. So it's always been God's intention for us to have his Word as a way of discerning truth from error, so it stands in a very high place in our minds.

Let me look at a couple of quick verses just to emphasize natural revelation, probably both very familiar to you. Psalm 19. It's a very common one.

David says:

> The heavens declare the glory of God,
>   and the sky above proclaims his handiwork.
> Day to day pours out speech,
>   and night to night reveals knowledge.
> There is no speech, nor are there words,
>   whose voice is not heard.
> Their voice goes out through all the earth,

and their words to the end of the world.[6]

And that sounds a little like what the Apostle says in the first chapter of Romans, isn't it? What does he say there? Romans 1, verse 20:

> For [God's] invisible attributes, namely, his eternal power and divine nature, have been clearly perceived, ever since the creation of the world, in the things that have been made.[7]

So we have that idea of natural revelation. There is no one, as Paul will say, who has an excuse for not believing in God because he is revealed in the things that are made.

Let me also share with you an excerpt from the *Westminster Confession of Faith*, which is our doctrinal standard in the PCA.

Coming from the first chapter:

> The authority of the holy Scripture, for which it ought to be believed and obeyed, dependeth not upon the testimony of any man or church, but wholly upon God (who is truth itself), the Author thereof; and therefore it is to be received, because it is the Word of God.[8]

---

[6] Ps 19:1-4a (ESV).
[7] Rom 1:20a (ESV).
[8] *Westminster Confession of Faith*, Chapter 1.4.

And yet from the very beginning, what we see is man, rather than receiving the word of God, doing *what*? Judging it, evaluating it, and rejecting it.

<u>Antithesis and Dichotomy from the First Verse</u>

Now, we could ask this question. I've talked a little about the idea of antithesis—things that are opposites—things that cannot both be true at the same time and in the same relationship. I want to throw out another word for you, *dichotomy*. It's another one of those Greek words, isn't it? And it basically means to divide something into two. So a dichotomy would be that we're going to divide this assembly, right down the middle—we have those people on this side and those people on that side. The two of them together include everyone. So we've divided it into two parts. And we see dichotomy, for example, in regard to the relationship between truth and error. It's either true or it's not true. Or we could say in terms of morality, it's either right or it's wrong. So that's another important concept that we need to deal with and we're going to deal with it pretty quickly because where do we see the first illustration of *antithesis* and *dichotomy* in the scripture? Yeah, the very first verse, isn't that something? *In the beginning*, okay, where's the dichotomy there? There's a *beginning* and then there's a *before the beginning*. Or we could say there is a *time* and there is an *eternity*. *God created the heavens and the earth*. Well, let's just take *God created*. There's a distinction between *God* who creates and the *creation* that he creates. And *the heavens and the earth*, a distinction even within the created realm. We start to see the distinction between what we might call *terra firma* and the *sky* or the *heavens*.

So we start to see this right away and it goes throughout scripture and we're going to talk about how perhaps the greatest dichotomy of all is the dichotomy of salvation. There are only two endpoints in eternity, *heaven* and *hell*. The scripture doesn't permit any other. There's no annihilationism. There's no salvation after death. There is either *salvation* or *judgment*. And so from the very first verse to the very last verse, scripture is dealing with these kinds of things. And if we don't have a grasp on basic reason, then we're not going to be able to understand things very clearly.

The Source of All Confusion

Now we could ask the question, *what is the source of all confusion?* And there's a little hint there. There's someone in scripture who's referred to as *the father of lies*. That would be Satan, who shows up in chapter 3. So where there's clarity, where there's truth, where there's reason, as God has established creation from the very beginning, Satan shows up and interrupts the beauty and the perfection of this world that God has created. And he does it very simply by introducing doubt.

Now, it's kind of funny as I think about the irony of those in much of Christendom who don't want to defend Genesis 1. What are they really saying? *Has God said, I created the heavens and the earth in six days?* Well, yes, he has. Does he tell us exactly *how* he did that? No, he gives us something of a process. It's a very orderly process. If he does it in a certain way, there's probably a certain reason why he does it that way. And we should expect to find answers like that if we consider those questions. But the question of whether he created the heavens and the earth in six days is settled in Genesis chapter 1. And we'll talk when we get to the session on creation about how foolish it is for us to try to guess or try to invent what we think might have happened so long ago and so far back in time when there was literally no one there—no person there to see it. As Ken Ham says, there was one witness to creation and that was God and he told us how he did it. I might add to that, that I think that the angels were there and were witnesses to creation as well. But other than that, there was no *man* there to see exactly how it happened or exactly how long it took. And in that case, we have to rely on the testimony of the one who says this is how he did it. And because Genesis is historical and not poetical, there is no reason to try to distort the meaning of Genesis 1 to mean something else. So we take God's word as he delivers it to us, whereas Satan comes in and starts to put a stick in the creek (so to speak) and stir the mud and dirty the water and make it harder for us to understand seemingly what frankly five minutes ago was very clear. So we have to watch out for him and we'll think a little bit during the course of the day about how he does what he does. But the clue is—if you pay some particular attention to those opening verses of Genesis 3—you'll begin to see what his tactics are. And the tactics don't change very much. But he is crafty, and depending on which translation you have, it may say that he's the most *subtle* creature, or the *craftiest* of the creatures. He's very intelligent. We're also going to find out later that he knows exactly what God said. I think part of the necessity of saying there were angels at the beginning of creation is that Satan was there when God gave the command. He heard exactly what God said to the man. And yet he took what God said and started to distort it and cause doubt and confusion.

Where else do we see, or where do we see Satan quoting scripture? He's a crafty beast. In the wilderness when Christ is tempted. He's quoting from Psalm 91 and saying, *throw yourself off the temple because it is written, he will give his angels charge over you to bear you up so that you don't dash your foot against a stone.* And what does Jesus say in reply? *It is also written, you shall not put the Lord your God to the test.* And there becomes an important principle of interpretation. We're Reformed so we have a fancy Latin name for everything. In this case it's *analogia scriptura*—meaning that we compare scripture to scripture. That we can't just take little verses here and there and try to make them mean what we want them to say, but we have to take the *whole* of scripture. And so we need to be concerned not just with a few of the things that God has said, but all of it. He's revealed all of it for faith and for life.

Scripture Plus Skepticism Equals Liberalism (Mystical "God Words")

What happens then when we take scripture and add a dose of skepticism to it? We end up with something called *theological liberalism*. And I remember some years ago—when we were engaged in the pro-life battle—that one of the things that appeared by a columnist in our local newspaper was a statement (a church-going, by the way, church-going columnist, ostensibly) was a statement something like this: *We know what God's word says, we just don't know what it means*. And that's really a profoundly foolish statement, but it also basically says that even though you have about 800,000 words in this book that God has spoken, we have no idea what he said. We can't make any sense out of it. He tried. He gave it the old college try—a thousand pages, even in a slimline Bible—but he just couldn't make his point. Do we really believe that? If that's going to be our attitude towards scripture, then we really are lost. And man left to his own devices—it doesn't turn out well.

Just as a footnote, you can refer to the Enlightenment as an illustration of how poorly it goes when man says, *we are going by the powers of our own reason*, using man as the measure of himself to figure out what's true and what's not. And over the course of the history of philosophy these last few hundred years, if you wonder why we're in the state that we're in now, where the state of philosophy basically says, there's nothing that's true, there's nothing that we can know, epistemology is dead, there's no such thing as morality, ethics, that's all gone, we don't know what's true, we're completely lost. And so you see the kind of chaos and anarchy that results from that when we have abandoned truth and reason.

You're going to hear me quote a few times during the day from Francis Schaeffer. If there's someone who understood the flow of history and philosophy and where it was taking us and where we would end up better than Schaeffer, I haven't found him. I was recently rereading some of his works. It's funny that I keep looking back to the copyright page and saying, *when was this published? 1970? Really?* Because it sounds like it was written yesterday. I won't call him a prophet, but he was prophetic in his ability to see where the flow of philosophy and these ideas was taking us. He knew very well back in the 60s and early 70s where humanism was taking us, and here we are. And while it's alarming how quickly things have changed and gone south, it's not really surprising if we understand that the foundation of Christian thinking, the foundation of truth and reason—and we might add morality into that as well—was stripped away generations ago. We've been coasting on momentum and now things are grinding to a halt and this is where we are.

At any rate, I did have a point, and it was that Francis Schaeffer refers to this problem of theological liberalism as *God words*. He says, we use these God words, like *God* and like *Jesus*, but they don't mean anything. They're mystical words. Christianity has been turned into mysticism where there's really no truth. It's just whatever you want it to be. And he makes the point that there's no significant difference in terms of thinking between the secular philosophy of humanism and the theological liberalism that has *God words* rather than *God's truth*. And that's where we are, not only in society but also in much of the church, unfortunately.

If it's the case that God cannot speak clearly, then we are in serious trouble. Because the scripture claims a number of things for itself. One of the things that it claims—well, here's a *for instance*—it claims to be *true*. That's kind of important. It claims to be precisely the word of God. And if it's *true*, and it is the word of *God*, then guess what? It comes with *authority*. And if God says, *this is my law*, it's not up for debate. And yet the whole history of civilization since the Fall has been one of rebelling against the word of God, as he's revealed it to us—and suffering the consequences.

I can't help thinking about the anecdote of the ox kicking against the goads. In one of Paul's testimonies of his conversion, he says, *the Lord said to him, it is hard for you to kick against the goads*. And that refers to a board with spikes in it that was placed behind the stubborn ox as it's pulling the cart. The ox would kick backwards into this board full of spikes, and all he's doing is hurting himself. He's not really accomplishing anything. He's only showing how stubborn he is, even to the point of causing himself pain. And that's much like what the human heart is in its fallen condition. We will kick against God's truth. We will kick against his law and say, *no, I'm going to do this my way*. And the results are disastrous.

Only Two Destinations

Now as we bring this session to a conclusion, I want to turn your attention to chapter 16 of Luke. There is a narrative in Luke 16, and I won't call it a *parable* because it's not quite clear if it's a parable or if it's an actual historical event. But it involves a rich man and a poor beggar named Lazarus. So I would like to read that section of scripture to you starting in verse 19.

"There was a rich man who was clothed in purple and fine linen and who feasted sumptuously every day. And at his gate was laid a poor man named Lazarus, covered with sores, who desired to be fed with what fell from the rich man's table. Moreover, even the dogs came and licked his sores. The poor man died and was carried by the angels to Abraham's side. The rich man also died and was buried, and in Hades, being in torment, he lifted up his eyes and saw Abraham far off and Lazarus at his side. And he called out, 'Father Abraham, have mercy on me, and send Lazarus to dip the end of his finger in water and cool my tongue, for I am in anguish in this flame.' But Abraham said, 'Child, remember that you in your lifetime received your good things, and Lazarus in like manner bad things; but now he is comforted here, and you are in anguish. And besides all this, between us and you a great chasm has been fixed, in order that those who would pass from here to you may not be able, and none may cross from there to us.' And he said, 'Then I beg you, father, to send him to my father's house—for I have five brothers—so that he may warn them, lest they also come into this place of torment.' But Abraham said, 'They have Moses and the Prophets; let them hear them.' And he said, 'No, father Abraham, but if someone goes to them from the dead, they will repent.' He said to him, 'If they do not hear Moses and the Prophets, neither will they be convinced if someone should rise from the dead.'"[9]

And here I'll make a quick point, going back to the opening idea of truth and reason. If you've ever wondered why it is that you can argue with someone and no amount of *persuasion*, no amount of *information*, no amount of *data* will change their mind. This helps us to understand

---

[9] Luke 16:19-31 (ESV).

what it means that when we worship idols, we become *blind*. We can't even see what's in front of us.

What's this story describing? Two men, one who lived, frankly, a miserable life. Sick, sore, unable to care for himself, looking for just a little compassion. And then this rich man. Now what's interesting about this is that you might have expected the sick man to die. That wouldn't be too much of a surprise. But what happens is the one who wasn't sick also died. And it sounds like they died at about the same time. Death almost certainly came as a surprise to the rich man in his comfort. And what do we infer from this story about where the rich man expected to be after he died? It's pretty clear that he did not expect to be in the flame. And yet he lived in comfort without regard for the life to come. He was concerned about the things of this life and obviously not concerned about the things of the next. And then his plea, part of his plea is, *let me go back and warn my brothers*. I don't want them to end up in the same place because they must be thinking the same thing that I was, that heaven is where they're going to end up. But it's not. And we see that salvation is not by works, it's not by status or wealth, power, any of those kinds of things. That both the *rich* man and the *poor* man die. That the one who's *well* and the one who's *sick*, they both die. And that the real question that we're left with is *where do we end up after we die?* And here's both the *dichotomy* and the *antithesis*.

There's a heaven and there's a hell. Those are the only two options. And so it's incumbent upon us—and part of the lesson of this narrative is that after you die there is no changing the equation. That the matter of salvation has to be settled in this life. And so throughout the day I'm going to be urging you with words like this to consider the state of your own salvation and to remember what God has done in Christ for your salvation, and to put your trust in him, because he is the only way and the only truth.

Let me finish briefly with a quote from R.C. Sproul—one of my favorites.

> When there's something in the Word of God that I don't like, the problem is not with the Word of God, it's with me.

Amen.

Session 2: The God Who Is

Scripture (Gen 1:1-3)

> In the beginning, God created the heavens and the earth. The earth was without form and void, and darkness was over the face of the deep. And the Spirit of God was hovering over the face of the waters. And God said, "Let there be light," and there was light.[10]

Introduction

A number of years ago, I worked with a man who expressed what is probably a common view of the Bible. As we were talking one day in his office he said to me, *I believe the Bible was inspired by God but it was written by men who make mistakes.* At the time, it happens that his wife was an assistant pastor at the PCUSA church here in Lufkin. So I had an inkling right away about the kind of "mistakes" he would probably find in the Bible. Perhaps I should have asked him to give me a list just to press the point. We have to understand that it creates an intractible problem if we say we can't trust what the Bible says. Now what is the standard? And the answer should be obvious just as it was in the case of Adam and Eve. The standard is *yourself*—what you like or what you don't like, what you think sounds reasonable or what you think might

---

[10] Gen 1:1-3 (ESV).

be unreasonable, the kinds of morals and ethics that you agree with and perhaps those that you strongly disagree with. Things that might get in the way of you living the way you want to. That's a problem because now if we admit to the possibility that there's even *one* error in scripture—and that it can no longer serve as the perfect standard for what's true—we're in trouble because *now we don't have a standard at all*. Think about what it would be like even if there were *one* mistake in the scripture. How would we know it? And if it were the case that we said there's one mistake somewhere in scripture but we don't know where it is, then what would our attitude be about the rest of the Bible? How could we know that we could rely on what it says? And it's fitting to ask that kind of question with regard to the book of Genesis. Because if we say, well, *Genesis 1 is mythology, we know it didn't really happen that way, science tells us something different*, then we're undermining the truth of scripture from the very first verse.

So it was important for us in that first session to establish the necessity of truth and reason *before* we come to the word of God to see what it says, starting from the first verse, so that we know that we can make sense out of it and that we can receive it as we ought to, which is as the word of God, with authority. So what we're going to cover in this session is certainly not a comprehensive overview of the attributes of God. What I've intended to do here is draw some inferences. One of the things that our *Confession* says is that we believe what scripture says and what it reveals as well as what we can determine from what's called *necessary consequence*. If we read a verse that says this person called God created the heavens and the earth then the necessary consequence of that is that this must be a very powerful person. It's that kind of an idea. So the question is, as we begin to look at the first chapter of Genesis, *what kinds of things can we already begin to see about the nature of this God who is the Creator?* So I've picked out five, and it's somewhat coincidental or happenstance, you might say, that I ended up alliterating these five. It just happened. I really wasn't trying to do that.

The five that I'd like to think about in this session are, first of all, the *pre-existence* of God, the *power* of God, the *purpose* of God, the *personality* of God. And before you jump to the wrong conclusion about what I mean by personality, I'm not talking about whether he's got a sense of humor or not, you know, what his favorite color is, or that kind of thing. I'm talking about the *personhood* of God, that he is a *personal* God. In fact, we're going to see that he's more than personal. He ends up being what we call *tri-personal* in the three persons of the Trinity. So personality, and then lastly, *promises*. We're already starting to see very early on that God relates to man through promises, or what we call *covenants*. So covenants are an important idea from the very beginning of scripture.

And lastly, as we close this session, we'll talk about a confrontation that took place on Mars Hill between Paul and the Greeks. And I selected that particular passage to conclude this session because we're going to see an illustration of how Paul appeals to God as the *Creator*—the Creator and the sustainer of all things. And as we think about the importance of Genesis and we think about the controversy over creation, it's not a small thing that God so often is described as the Creator. It's as if—*as if*—the scripture is reminding us that this God that we're talking about is the one who created everything. And it should bring to mind these kinds of attributes that we're going to spend a little time thinking about in this session.

The Pre-Existence of God

So we start with the first one, *pre-existence*. It's one of those philosophical ideas. And we can see that from the very first verse. *In the beginning, God created the heavens and the earth.* Well, what does that mean? There was a beginning to the heavens and the earth, and the beginning was brought about by a God who was already there. And how long has he been there? And the answer is, he has always been there. And that's what we mean by the idea of pre-existence. We talk about God being *eternal*. Now, eternal can have a couple of different meanings. If I say, for example, how long is your soul going to live?

You'll say, well, it's eternal. It's going to live forever. That's true, but it had a beginning. It may not have an *end* to its existence, but it had a *beginning*. And part of the distinction with God is that he had no beginning.

Now, if you're trying to describe the eternality of God in human language, when virtually everything we know and understand is what we say *temporal* or even *temporary*, that it has a time, it has a beginning and an end, and we think in terms of when something starts and when it ends and how it moves from one time to another, a *chronology*. And we start talking about eternity and it's a much more difficult concept. How do you measure eternity with a clock? And the answer is, you can't.

One of my favorite lines from The Chronicles of Narnia is at the end of one of the episodes where Aslan is saying goodbye to Lucy on the beach. I think it's next to Cair Paravel. And Lucy says, *well, when am I going to see you again?* And Aslan says, *soon.* And Lucy says, *well, when is soon?* And Aslan says, *for me, all times are soon.*[11]

---

[11] My memory of the conversation between Lucy and Aslan was a bit confused and it demonstrates the danger of making an illustration on the fly. This exchange took place in *The Voyage of the Dawn Treader* when Lucy went into the Magician's house on the Island of the Voices and there had a brief encounter with Aslan. It is found at the beginning of Chapter 11 in the book. It was not at the end of the episode, and it was nowhere near Cair Paravel. But now we both know.

How do you describe one who inhabits eternity, who knows all things in all times and all places comprehensively from beginning to end? We could say, for example, that it wasn't necessary for God to wait until a part of history had unfolded, until somebody named Moses came along and God began to reveal himself through his written word to a guy named Moses several thousand years after creation, because he's waiting to see how things are going—if things are going according to plan, if it's safe for him to start writing these things down. You understand, certainly, that God could have just as easily revealed the whole of scripture from beginning to end to Adam. In fact, scripture is described as being God's eternal Word, written in the heavens. So God inhabits eternity. He doesn't just determine history, he controls all of it. He doesn't just know it, but he has written it, literally, from the beginning, from before the beginning.

So there's this idea of God's pre-existence. It's captured in a couple of different ways. Let's take a look first of all in Psalm 90. I'm just going to read the first two verses, very short, but very powerful in terms of what it says. And this happens to be, by the way, the psalm that Moses wrote in the wilderness.

> Lord, you have been our dwelling place
>   in all generations.
> Before the mountains were brought forth,

> or ever you had formed the earth and the world,
> from everlasting to everlasting you are God.[12]

And how is it that this God describes himself when Moses asks him, *when I go to Pharaoh, what do I say? Who's sending me?* And God's answer is, *I am who I am.* I am—the eternal one, the everlasting one, without beginning or end.

We also see this idea captured in several different ways in the book of Revelation, and I'll direct your attention to a few short passages. Take a look at verse 17 and following. We're in chapter 1 of Revelation. John says:

> When I saw him, I fell at his feet as though dead. But he laid his right hand on me, saying, "Fear not . . ."

And this is Christ speaking, the risen Christ who is appearing to John on the island of Patmos.

> "Fear not, I am the first and the last, and the living one. I died, and behold I am alive forevermore, and I have the keys of Death and Hades."[13]

We also see in verse 8:

---

[12] Psalm 90:1-2 (ESV).
[13] Rev 1:17-18 (ESV).

> "I am the Alpha and the Omega," says the Lord God, "who is and who was and who is to come, the Almighty."[14]

And we'll see how in Genesis, God reveals himself as the Almighty. You often see that word, which is the translation of El Shaddai, the Almighty One. And here's where I'm going to take a little swipe at the translation. *I am the Alpha and the Omega*. What does that mean? Well, those are the first and the last letters of the Greek alphabet. The English translation might say, *I am the A and the Z, the beginning and the end*. He's trying to express this idea that from whatever span that you can try to describe, whether it's in terms of time or whether it's in terms of knowledge, using the alphabet here as an example, that he covers the whole spectrum from beginning to end. There was never a time when God was not.

Now there's some satisfying scientific consequences about that. There's something in the world of science called the Law of Causality. And the Law of Causality is not that *everything* has a cause. The Law of Causality is that every *effect* has a cause. And there was a time not too long ago when the scientific community understood that something had to be eternal. If you go back 100 years or so, the cosmological paradigm was that the universe has existed eternally. And that was a better answer than the answer that we have today, because now that we have shifted

---

[14] Rev 1:8 (ESV).

the paradigm into what's called Big Bang cosmology—the idea that there was a beginning—then the obvious question is, *what happened before the beginning?* Where did the stuff come from if there was a beginning to the universe? And in typical irrational and dishonest fashion, the scientist is going to look you in the eye and say, *it came from nothing.* The universe created itself from nothing. That really is the answer that you get. Even someone like Stephen Hawking believed in this idea of self-creation, which is a logical absurdity because nothing can create itself. As R.C. Sproul used to say, *if there was ever a time when there was nothing, then what would you have now? Nothing.* Because nothing creates nothing.

Now, I'm not a fan of Big Bang cosmology. I'll explain a little more about that later when we get further down the road. I would warn you as a way of preview that as a Christian you shouldn't latch on to whatever science said yesterday or today because tomorrow it's probably going to change. Science is highly fallible and it is never immutable, because it never really *proves* anything. It makes observations and draws conclusions. The conclusions are often wrong, but they may stand for some time until we come up with a better idea. Logically, though, the necessary existence of an eternal Creator is looming there. We can't escape it. And so we have this idea of God being pre-existent or everlasting—eternal, as we would say.

Let me direct you to one or two other verses while we're here in Revelation. We also see, for example, in verse 8 of chapter 2, where he says:

> "And to the angel of the church in Smyrna write: 'The words of the first and the last. . . .'"[15]

So again we have this recurring idea of God being the first and last and we can see that again over in the very last chapter of Revelation if you'd like to flip over there. Jesus says:

> "Behold, I am coming soon, bringing my recompense with me, to repay each one for what he has done. I am the Alpha and the Omega, the first and the last, the beginning and the end."[16]

And with those kinds of expressions, we virtually exhaust what human language can do to explain what it means for God to be eternal.

Let me point you also, flip back to 1 Timothy, chapter 1. In verse 17, Paul engages in a little doxology here when he says:

> To the King of the ages, immortal, invisible, the only God, be honor and glory forever and ever. Amen.[17]

---

[15] Rev 2:8 (ESV).
[16] Rev 22:12-13 (ESV).
[17] 1 Tim 1:17 (ESV).

And so over and over, scripture affirms this idea that God is eternal and immortal. We begin to see that from the very first verse of Genesis.

The Power of God

And what about his *power*? How much power does it take to create the universe? I thought about doing a little calculation, but I didn't follow through on that. But I imagine taking just a small rock that weighs perhaps just a few ounces and saying, what would happen if we could take this rock, which is completely nondescript, and in an instant convert it into pure energy? If we could take all, just a little bit of mass in a small rock and convert it into pure energy, what would happen? I'm pretty sure it would wipe out most of the country because of that relationship that Einstein famously delivered to us, $E = mc^2$. The energy that's contained in even a rock is the mass of the rock multiplied by the speed of light squared, which the speed of light is already a pretty big number. And you take a really big number and you square it and it's a really, really big number.

So just reflect on this idea for a moment. How much energy does God have to expend even to create a little rock that you can hold in your hands? I think there is in that idea—this connection between mass and energy—that God is so powerful that he can expend all the energy that's necessary to create all the mass of the known universe, trillions and trillions and trillions of tons of mass, and all virtually in an instant. And oh, by the way, it didn't make him tired when he did that. He was not the least bit spent in terms of his own energy when he did that, because his power is infinite. We can't comprehend this, and yet we begin to see the hints of it even in the very first verse of Genesis where God creates the heavens and the earth. Of course, Genesis goes on to unfold the rest of creation as God continues to finish out the work, so to speak. And we'll later see, as Genesis unfolds, that he's not just creating rocks, not just creating an earth or a sea or a sky, but that the point of his creation is to bring life into this world. That he is not just powerful, but that he is the source of all life. He's first of all, we would say that first of all he is the source of all being because there would be nothing here if there weren't God. But he's also the source of life because nothing that exists would have life if God did not give it life. And that's an entirely different kind of creation. It's the kind of thing that science really doesn't even try to explain because it can't. We could put it this way, that there is no natural law that explains how life comes out of something that's inanimate. And yet God does this over and over again as he fills out the creation in this first chapter of Genesis.

And what does it take for him to do that, by the way? What is the recurring theme? What do we see in verse 3? *And God said, let there be* light. *And there was light.* All it takes is the power of the Word for God to create all things. And that's a remarkable thing.

So as we talk about the power of this God, I'm going to point you to another passage in Genesis 18. And I'd like to look at verses 9 through 15 of Genesis 18. It's a familiar story. Abraham and Sarah are old. God appears to Abraham and says to him, *about this time next year you're going to have a child.* And, of course, Sarah overhears that conversation and her response is laughter— *Yitschâq,* and that becomes his name. And there's somebody here in the audience whose son is named Isaac. He might have taken more jesting in school if you had named him Laughter. But that is precisely his name, Laughter. Because why? It seems absurd that a woman who's 90 years old and a man who's 100 years old could conceive a child. And yet, as God is describing this to Abraham, what does he say? Referring to the angels that came to visit him:

They said to him, "Where is Sarah your wife?"

I'm in verse 9.

> And he said, "She is in the tent." The LORD said, "I will surely return to you about this time next year, and Sarah your wife shall have a son." And Sarah was listening at the tent door behind him. Now Abraham and Sarah were old, advanced in

years. The way of women had ceased to be with Sarah. So Sarah laughed to herself, saying, "After I am worn out, and my lord is old, shall I have pleasure?" The LORD said to Abraham, "Why did Sarah laugh and say, 'Shall I indeed bear a child, now that I am old?'"

Verse 14. This is the rhetorical question:

"Is anything too hard for the LORD? At the appointed time I will return to you, about this time next year, and Sarah shall have a son." But Sarah denied it, saying, "I did not laugh," for she was afraid. He said, "No, but you did laugh."[18]

Sarah laughs again at the birth of Isaac. And we probably would be inclined to think that, at that time, it was a laughter of joy at the birth of her child, even though it's a laughter of a little scorn at this time, thinking, *how could I possibly have a child at this age?* And yet the Lord simply says, by way of a question, *is there anything that I can't do?* And what's the answer? We don't need the answer, do we? The answer for the one who is Almighty is that he can do anything. He can do whatever he chooses to do.

I'd also like you to turn over to the book of Daniel. We'll look at a passage from there as well. And this is an interesting passage for a couple of reasons. You'll recall that—Daniel 4—you'll recall that a king

---

[18] Gen 18:9-15 (ESV).

named Nebuchadnezzar was warned about his pride. He was given a somber warning that if he didn't check his pride that the Lord was going to humble him. And sometime afterward the Lord did humble him. And how did the Lord humble him on that occasion? He made him insane. He basically made him behave as if he were a cow, crawling around on all fours, growing long hair and fingernails, acting like a beast, losing his sensibility, literally. And so where we pick up this narrative, is at the end of that. Let me go back just a couple of verses here. Let me go back to verse 33 where it says:

> Immediately the word was fulfilled against Nebuchadnezzar. He was driven from among men and ate grass like an ox, and his body was wet with the dew of heaven till his hair grew as long as eagles' feathers, and his nails were like birds' claws.[19]

This is not a pretty picture, but this insanity of Nebuchadnezzar is a judgment, and it's a judgment against his pridefulness for thinking that he was great. What was it that prompted this? We don't have to go back very far to see this. Take a look at verse 30.

> "Is not this great Babylon, which I have built by my mighty power as a royal residence and for the glory of my majesty?"[20]

---

[19] Dan 4:33 (ESV).
[20] Dan 4:30 (ESV).

So here it comes. He spends seven years acting like a beast. And God restores his senses and restores his kingdom. And the evidence seems to suggest that not only he was restored, but that when he came back to his senses, he was a true believer in the God of Israel. Verse 34:

> At the end of the days I, Nebuchadnezzar, lifted my eyes to heaven, and my reason returned to me, and I blessed the Most High, and praised and honored him who lives forever,
>
> for his dominion is an everlasting dominion,
>   and his kingdom endures from generation to generation;
> all the inhabitants of the earth are accounted as nothing,
>   and he does according to his will among the host of heaven
>   and among the inhabitants of the earth;
> and none can stay his hand
>   or say to him, "What have you done?"[21]

What does that tell us about the power of God, the *omnipotence* of God as we describe it? That he has the power to do whatever he purposes to do. And that raises one of those interesting theological questions, such as, *can God make a rock that's so big he can't move it?* And the answer is *no*. I would put it like this, that God, by virtue of what he does, cannot handcuff himself. If he makes creation a certain way, to operate a certain way, according to what we call *natural laws*, does that constrain

---
[21] Dan 4:34-35 (ESV).

him from acting against it or acting with it? And the answer is *no*. He can do as he pleases, just as Nebuchadnezzar observed.

So this power of God first appears to us in his creation, simply bringing everything into existence. There's another Latin word for that, *ex nihilo*, that refers to bringing creation into existence out of nothing. In other words, it's not like a potter who sits down at the potter's wheel and grabs a lump of clay and starts to shape it. God didn't have a chair. He didn't have a potter's wheel. He didn't have clay. He had to make all of those things first. So he starts creating out of nothing. And again, that gives us just a glimpse into the power of this God who creates.

The Purpose of God

Now, what about his *purpose*? God has a purpose in everything that he does. It wouldn't make sense to say, here's this almighty, all-wise, all-powerful God who just acts arbitrarily. Or he starts to do something, but he doesn't really know what he's going to do as time goes by. We may do that. We may start a project and say, *I'm not sure where this is going to go or when I'm going to finish or how it's going to turn out, but I'm going to go ahead and start it anyway*. God never does that. He can't do that. Whatever he does, he must do with the plan and the purpose in mind ahead of time. Again, the idea is that he inhabits eternity. He knows the end that he's designed for his creation. And he has the power to direct everything toward that end, whether acting *with* the creation—what we call *providence*—or whether acting *against* it, which is what we call a *miracle*.

We see the drama of redemption already starting to unfold even at the very beginning of Genesis, though by the time we get to end of chapter 2, everything looks pretty good. God says *it's all very good*. Nothing has intruded into this perfect creation yet. It's about to, and the story is going to take what we might call a dark turn in chapter 3. But again, is God surprised by what happens in the Fall? And the answer is no. He's already provided for that. He's already planned for that. And that's going to be what begins to expose, to reveal his redemptive plan.

What we see in part from the order of creation—and again this is completely contrary to what science would tell us—is that he begins with the heavens and the earth and then he starts to give it shape and form, separating land from water, and then he begins to bring life into it, little by little. He begins to add, you might say, the icing on the cake. It's interesting if you're a fan of cosmology or astronomy, that it simply says on day four, and *he created the stars also*. Billions and billions of stars. Just *created the stars also*. But the best is yet to come. Because at the end of day six, what's he going to do? The culminating achievement of this creative work is to make man and to make man *in his image*. And to make man in such a way that man will be in relationship with God.

The Personality of God

There's not a relationship *per se* between plants and animals and God except that they are part of his creation. But now we're talking again about the idea that God has *personality*, that he not only has personality within himself, but he has personality that can relate personally to his creatures.

Now, don't we already see some hints of the Trinity in chapter 1 of Genesis? In the very opening verses, in fact, it's almost as if I selected those first three verses with that point in mind:

> In the beginning, God created the heavens and the earth. The earth was without form and void, and darkness was over the face of the deep. And the Spirit of God was hovering over the face of the waters. And God said, "Let there be light," and there was light.[22]

Well, we have the Spirit described very explicitly, separately from God, seemingly. We have God—by the way, you may know that Hebrew word *Elohim* is a plural form of the word *El*, which refers to God. We're

---

[22] Gen 1:1-3 (ESV).

already getting a hint that there's more than one person in what we will call the Godhead. So we have the *Spirit* of God, and then God said, *let there be light*. Now this is a twofer, if I wanted to be a little cheeky about it. Because what is God's *word*? Or should I say, *who* is God's Word? And interestingly, as we look at the parallel between those opening verses and the opening verses in the Gospel of John, we suspect that there's a connection there, don't we? When John says:

> In the beginning was the Word, and the Word was *with* God, and the Word *was* God. He was in the beginning *with* God.

And then verse 3:

> All things were made through him, and without him was not any thing made that was made. In him was life, and the life was the light of men. The light shines in the darkness, and the darkness has not overcome it.[23]

We see *God*, we see *Spirit*, we see the *Word* and the *Light*, and the reference back to Genesis 1 is unmistakable. John often refers to Jesus as the Light that has come into the world, and the Word, what's called the *Logos*. And it's an interesting little detail that in the Greek Septuagint at the beginning of Genesis, the translation is *Logos*, that there is that connection with God and his *Word* and his Spirit.

---

[23] John 1:1-5 (ESV).

So we're already seeing this very early in the book of Genesis and if we continue on we have a couple of other hints. What's another hint there in chapter 1 that there's more to this God than what we would call Unitarianism? Look at verse 26:

> Then God said, "Let *us* make man in *our* image, after *our* likeness."[24]

Once again, a hint that there is something more to God than just a single personality. I thought about it like this. This gives you an idea of how I think. I sit at home and talk to myself all the time. Maybe I shouldn't tell you that. In fact, lately I've been sitting at home thinking about what I was going to say, and doing a little practice, you might say, of what I would say when I came to speak to you. So was I really talking to you if I was sitting at my desk and trying to picture this group in front of me? No, because you weren't there. Was I talking to myself? It raises an interesting question: can I talk to myself? And the answer is no, not really. Because I don't have a self to talk to. If I'm talking, then I'm not listening. If I'm listening, I'm not talking. There's only one of me. And yet, does it make more sense when God says, *let us make man in our image after our likeness?* There's this idea of an inter-Trinitarian conversation. Can God talk to himself? And the answer is, *well, yes he can.*

---

[24] Gen 1:26a (ESV).

I've got an even better one than that. Can God *love* himself? Where is God's love most perfectly expressed? In the Trinity, between the members of the Trinity. And so you could make this argument that there's this necessity of God having more than a single personal nature for him to be able to, first of all, talk to himself, but also to be able to relate to a creature. So it's remarkable that we begin to see by hints, but unmistakable hints, in the opening chapter of Genesis that there's something more to this God than just what we would think of a single personality.

The Promises of God

Next we can think in terms of his *promises*. And here I'd like to quote briefly again from the *Westminster Confession*—this time from chapter 7.

I'm going to start at the beginning of Chapter 7 in the *Westminster Confession*. And this is the chapter of God's covenant with man.

> The distance between God and the creature is so great that although reasonable creatures do owe obedience unto him as their Creator, yet they could never have any fruition of him as their blessedness and reward but by some voluntary

> condescension on God's part, which he hath been pleased to express by way of covenant.[25]

> The first covenant made with man was a covenant of works, wherein life was promised to Adam, and in him to his posterity, upon condition of perfect and personal obedience.[26]

And then as we'll see a little later,

> Man by his fall having made himself incapable of life by that covenant, the Lord was pleased to make a second, commonly called the covenant of grace: wherein he freely offered unto sinners life and salvation by Jesus Christ, requiring of them faith in him that they may be saved, and promising to give unto all those that are ordained unto life his Holy Spirit, to make them willing and able to believe.[27]

It's remarkable that we see, from the very beginning, God establishing a covenant, a relationship with his creatures and that through his promises.

One of the things we'll see when we start to talk a little more about the image of God in man, is that we see already that there's a very special relationship between God and this creature called man. And this covenant or this promise is what begins to make that possible.

---

[25] *Westminster Confession of Faith*, Chapter 7.1.
[26] *Westminster Confession of Faith*, Chapter 7.2.
[27] *Westminster Confession of Faith*, Chapter 7.3.

The Confrontation on Mars Hill

Now as we bring this session to a close, I'd like to turn your attention to the book of Acts again, this time in chapter 17.

So this is Paul giving his testimony at the Areopagus. Verse 22:

> So Paul, standing in the midst of the Areopagus, said: "Men of Athens, I perceive that in every way you are very religious. For as I passed along and observed the objects of your worship . . ."

It was a city full of idols.

> ". . . I found also an altar with this inscription: 'To the unknown god.'"

That becomes his point of contact and his point of launching into the gospel.

> "What therefore you worship as unknown, this I proclaim to you. The God who made the world and everything in it, being Lord of heaven and earth, does not live in temples made by man, nor is he served by human hands, as though he needed anything, since he himself gives to all mankind life and breath and everything. And he made from one man [Adam] every nation of mankind to live on all the face of the earth, having determined allotted periods and the boundaries of their

dwelling place, that they should seek God, and perhaps feel their way toward him and find him. Yet he is actually not far from each one of us, for

"'In him we live and move and have our being';

as even some of your own poets have said,

"'For we are indeed his offspring.'"[28]

Paul is starting where he's at, so to speak, in witnessing to the Athenians. And the first thing that he does is he demolishes their idols by pointing them to whom? The God who created the heavens and the earth in the beginning, the one who gives life, the one who sustains life.

If it's the case that God is the Creator, if it's the case that he is the only true God, then to him all allegiance is owed. All the other gods are gods of wood and stone, and you can dress them up any way you want to, you can call them whatever you want to, but they are mute. They cannot speak, they cannot hear, they cannot see. They have no power to do anything, not even to get themselves from one part of the room to the other. And so Paul is using that as the point of departure to tell them about this Creator God. *The one that you say that you don't know, let me tell you who he is.*

---

[28] Acts 17:22-28 (ESV).

Let me read on a little further, starting in verse 29:

> "Being then God's offspring, we ought not to think that the divine being is like gold or silver or stone, an image formed by the art and imagination of man. The times of ignorance God overlooked, but now he commands all people everywhere to repent, because he has fixed a day on which he will judge the world in righteousness by a man whom he has appointed; and of this he has given assurance to all by raising him from the dead."[29]

Now there's so much that we could unpack in that. But it serves as both an offer and a warning. We have often lived in times of ignorance, ignorant unbelief, following after gods of wood and stone, following after our own desires. And here Paul is saying there is one who is appointed to judge the whole world. And he's also appointed to be the Savior of mankind. And the manner in which we approach this Jesus will determine what the end is for us, whether an end of joy in heaven or whether an end of judgment in hell.

John Calvin has this to say regarding scripture:

> We owe to Scripture the same reverence that we owe to God because it has proceeded from Him alone and has nothing belonging to man mixed with it.

---

[29] Act 17:29-31 (ESV).

Over and over again the scripture says of itself that it is *pure*, it is *clean*, it is *perfect*. And we are to turn to that for the knowledge that's required to lay hold of salvation through Christ.

Amen.

Session 3: Creation from Nothing

Scripture (Gen 1:1-25)

In the beginning, God created the heavens and the earth. The earth was without form and void, and darkness was over the face of the deep. And the Spirit of God was hovering over the face of the waters.

And God said, "Let there be light," and there was light. And God saw that the light was good. And God separated the light from the darkness. God called the light Day, and the darkness he called Night. And there was evening and there was morning, the first day.

And God said, "Let there be an expanse in the midst of the waters, and let it separate the waters from the waters." And God made the expanse and separated the waters that were under the expanse from the waters that were above the expanse. And it was so. And God called the expanse Heaven. And there was evening and there was morning, the second day.

And God said, "Let the waters under the heavens be gathered together into one place, and let the dry land appear." And it was so. God called the dry land Earth, and the waters that were gathered together he called Seas. And God saw that it was good.

And God said, "Let the earth sprout vegetation, plants yielding seed, and fruit trees bearing fruit in which is their seed, each according to its kind, on the earth." And it was so. The earth brought forth vegetation, plants yielding seed according to their own kinds, and trees bearing fruit in which is their seed, each according to its kind. And God saw that it was good. And there was evening and there was morning, the third day.

And God said, "Let there be lights in the expanse of the heavens to separate the day from the night. And let them be for signs and for seasons, and for days and years, and let them be lights in the expanse of the heavens to give light upon the earth." And it was so. And God made the two great lights—the greater light to rule the day and the lesser light to rule the night—and the stars. And God set them in the expanse of the heavens to give light on the earth, to rule over the day and over the night, and to separate the light from the darkness. And God saw that it was good. And there was evening and there was morning, the fourth day.

And God said, "Let the waters swarm with swarms of living creatures, and let birds fly above the earth across the expanse of the heavens." So God created the great sea creatures and every living creature that moves, with which the waters swarm, according to their kinds, and every winged bird according to its kind. And God saw that it was good. And God blessed them, saying, "Be fruitful and multiply and fill the waters in the seas, and let birds multiply on the earth." And there was evening and there was morning, the fifth day.

And God said, "Let the earth bring forth living creatures according to their kinds—livestock and creeping things and beasts of the earth according to their kinds." And it was so. And God made the beasts of the earth according to their kinds and the livestock according to their kinds, and everything that creeps on the ground according to its kind. And God saw that it was good.[30]

---

[30] Gen 1:1-25 (ESV).

Session 3: Creation From Nothing

Introduction

As we start this session, I want to share something that I recently came across on YouTube. That's probably a dangerous thing to say because you can come across a lot of things on YouTube that aren't worth paying much attention to. But this was a bit of a composite video that took some snippets from two different people whose names you'd probably recognize and put them side by side in this little video. The names of the two people in this video are Andy Stanley and William Lane Craig, not to be confused with William *Neil* Craig, who is present today.[31] And what was alarming about this, and I was aware that William Lane Craig has a reputation as a Christian apologist. I do recall watching a debate of his some years ago. And I wasn't really impressed, frankly, because at the very beginning of the debate, he did what a presuppositional apologist would never do. He said to the person he was debating, *I'm willing to concede to you the laws of logic*. And I'm thinking, *you just lost the debate*. Because that is one of the most important presuppositions that you need to argue. And it comes from the Christian presuppositions and not from atheistic presuppositions. So I never paid that much attention to him as an apologist over the years until this video came across my list of suggested videos a couple weeks ago. And I watched it, and there's no surprise that Andy Stanley would

---

[31] This Bill Craig is an elder at Covenant Presbyterian Church.

stand up and declare that Genesis is a myth, that the creation story is a myth. This is the same guy who said a year or two ago that we don't need the Old Testament at all. So I'm not sure why he would even care whether Genesis is true or not.

But what surprised me was for Craig to say the same thing. And it really begs an important question, doesn't it? What is that? If you call yourself a defender of scripture, the obvious question is, where would you like to start? And if somebody's not willing to defend Genesis 1 or 2 or maybe 3—I don't know how far—that's the question, we don't know. If you say that Genesis 1 is a myth, then what about Genesis 2? Mythology or truth? Genesis 3, mythology or truth? Genesis 4, mythology or truth? Where does the truth begin in scripture if you're not willing for it to begin in the first verse of the first chapter? And where exactly do you begin your apologetic of Christianity if you're not going to begin it at the beginning? And to receive the word of God as true and authoritative, inerrant, infallible, all of those things. That exposes a real problem. What does it mean to be an apologist or a defender of Christian truth, Christian faith, if you're not going to start at the beginning?

And we can ask ourselves, why is that? Why does it seem to be the case that so many ostensibly Christian people—even those who say they're apologists of Christianity—are not willing to start with Genesis chapter 1? What is it that's drawn us away from the word of God? And of course the answer is that there's a lot of deception, what seem like plausible ideas about how things got started and how they developed over time and how long it took for that to happen, and so forth. And a key idea that I want you to have in your mind as you think about how do we reconcile Genesis chapter 1 with what we call "science"—and I'm putting air quotes around it at the moment—is that when we start to bring those two in proximity to each other, we have to notice something. There's a question of *authority* that comes into play. Which of those two words—which of those two *worldviews*, as Bill would put it—which of those two worldviews is authoritative over the other one? Because that's what it is. It is a conflict of *worldviews*, and I'm glad you made that point, because it fits very well in what we're thinking about right now. Evolution is not science. It's a *worldview*. I'll be more specific. It's a *religion*. And it's a religion that explicitly denies the existence of God. We call it *atheism*. Is it surprising that if you start with the presupposition of atheism and try to work your way through an explanation of how things got to be the way they are, and you compare that to what we find in scripture that begins with the presupposition of the eternal power and existence of God who creates with a purpose, that you're going to come to different conclusions? In fact, they're completely incompatible.

And I'm going to throw out another term for you to think very carefully about, because what we're actually doing is we're mixing two religions when we do that. And the word is *syncretism*. And here's a way to think about it. I think it was John MacArthur who said something like this, that *when you take the truth and mix error with it, it doesn't get better.* Mixing truth and error does not improve the truth at all. In fact, in the dichotomy between truth and error, if you have something that is perfectly true over here on this hand and something that's perfectly false on the other and say, *I think I'll take a little of this, falsehood over here and mix it in with the truth over on this side*, what do you end up with? You end up with untruth. There's no middle ground between truth and error. And as soon as you start mixing untruth with truth, you get error. And that's often part of the tactics of the Deceiver. This is part of his craftiness, his subtlety. He's going to say things that seem very plausible. And he's also going to rely on what may be a lot of truth, even quoting scripture and saying, *well, what about this?* but using it in the wrong way. So we have to be mindful of that sort of thing. That's really the big issue and the reason why we have to defend scripture from the first verse. It's like I mentioned with my anecdote in the last session, if there are errors in the word of God, then what's the standard? How are we ever going to know what is true? And if we're left to our own devices to figure out what's true, we're already in trouble.

Let me point this out before I forget about it and miss the opportunity to mention it. When Adam and Eve were confronted in the Garden of Eden with the deception of the Serpent, they were still perfect. Well, as we'll see a couple sessions further down the road, we're *not*. We're going to talk about the fallenness and what the Fall has done, what effect it's had on our minds and on our ability to reason, our ability to discern. Adam and Eve didn't have the defect of the Fall when they were confronted with a little bit of a lie, and they fell for it anyway. So we really need to be mindful of how important our powers of discernment are in an age when we really are surrounded by—or you might say, *immersed in*—all kinds of deception.

So based on that little introduction, you can gather that when it comes to apologetics, I don't mind starting with Genesis 1, chapter 1, verse 1, because there's no place else to start. If you're not going to start with Genesis 1:1, I'm inclined to say just pack your bags and go home because you're not an apologist. The Bible is true from the very first verse.

Now in this session I'm going to be talking a little more about science, *so-called*. And I say so-called because from one standpoint—if we just take a little etymology again—science is a word that means *knowledge*. What is science? It's the pursuit of knowledge or the pursuit of truth.

And there's a methodology behind that. How do we discover truth with something called science? And it's, frankly, a very slow and a very messy process. We'll talk a little more about that in a bit as the process goes. But here's where we're running into trouble. And if you haven't noticed over the last year and a half, it's been very troubling to see what I would almost describe as the death of science in real time. Because of the way data has been manipulated, the way the narrative has been manipulated, taking only bits and pieces of things, not looking at the whole picture, or perhaps jumping to certain conclusions that are not warranted from the data—those kinds of things. But measurement especially, I could be on my soapbox all day long about what has gone haywire just over the last year and a half with regard to measurement.[32] Because if we're going to use the *facts* of science, we need to measure things properly.

At the risk of getting too distracted, I'll give you an aside just to illustrate the point. When it comes to the question of climate change, you hear this narrative that the temperature of the Earth is increasing. And I run that statement through my scientific filters and I say, *how do you measure the temperature of the Earth? How could you even do that?* Now, I'll give you a simple illustration to show you how absurd it is.

---

[32] I'm referring to the ever-changing COVID narrative of 2020-2021—especially the manipulation of data by constant changes in the definition of the metrics.

Session 3: Creation From Nothing

How do you measure the temperature in this *room*? Oh, well, there's a thermostat on the wall back there. It has a thermometer in it. We could go back there and look at the number and see it says the temperature is such and such in this room. But is that the temperature in the *room*? Well, it's the temperature of that spot on the wall back there, but is that the temperature in the room? Because the temperature on this side of the room might be very different from the temperature on that side of the room. And how do we do that? Are we going to take one measurement and say, *oh, here's the number*? This is the number at this particular moment in time? Are we going to continue to collect data 24 hours a day? And then what are we going to do with it? How are we going to average it out to determine what is "*the* temperature"? It's not a simple matter. And so when you hear narratives regarding science that involve things that sound so certain, so absolute, they're not nearly as certain as you might think because something as seemingly simple as measuring the temperature in a room is a science unto itself.

I'll give you one more illustration of this point—something that you can do as your own little practical experiment. The next time you go to Walmart—or maybe one of the hardware stores, something like that—go into the garden center where they have all the thermometers, right? All kinds of thermometers. And just see if you can find two of them that agree with each other. It's not as simple as it sounds. So all that to say, that we have to be very careful about the pronouncements of science because they may sound very authoritative, they may sound very factual, they may indeed be using facts, but the facts that they're using in some cases, frankly, are fabricated by something called *proxy data*. Those are not real measurements. We don't know what the temperature was 800 years ago. We've only been taking temperature measurements for about the last 150 years. So you have to be careful of that. There needs to be some caution and some skepticism in regard to what science says, and of course that's what brings us to the question today.

No One Was There

What does science say about creation? What does science answer to the question, *how did we get here? What are we doing here? How did this all happen? How did it all get started? How did it progress?* And here's where I'm going to put on the hat of the secular scientist for just a moment. It's like Paul saying, if you'll forgive me, *I'm going to be a fool for just a moment.* Let's pretend as if it really is true that the universe is 15 billion years old. We'll play *what if*, OK? And then how long has man been here? Eh, a few thousand years. Who was around to see the beginning of creation? Well, we weren't here yet. Evolution hadn't done its thing. Now let me illustrate the absurdity of the question by asking you a personal question. What did you have for dinner last Wednesday night? And you say, well, *I don't remember*. I was there. I had something, I'm sure, but I don't remember what it was. And then I said, well, your task—if you're willing to accept it—is to go back and figure out what you had at dinner last Wednesday night. And you might be able to look at your shopping list or, there might be some clues. Maybe you got a text from your spouse, something like that. Some evidence that's left behind about what you had for dinner last Wednesday night.

Now, in my case as a bachelor, I'd just dig down to the bottom of the sink and see what's still on the plate. I could dig up some forensic evidence pretty quickly. But for the rest of us, it's harder. And think about how hard it is, the further we get away from a certain event, to determine what happened, even if it's just a few days ago and something that doesn't matter at all, like what you had for dinner last week. And then we come to this idea that the universe is 15 *billion* years old. And when a scientist starts telling you that it all came into being with something called a Big Bang, you stop and think about the fact that there was nobody around 15 billion years ago if, in fact, that is what happened.

There are different kinds of science. The two that we rely on the most are *observational* science and *experimental* science. I can go out here in the churchyard and observe how fast the grass is growing at this time of the year. I can measure that. I can measure it today and then I can come back in a day or two and measure it again and say the grass is growing at this rate. It's an observational measurement. Or if I said I want to find out just how fast St. Augustine grass will grow, I'm going to set up a controlled experiment where I create just the right conditions for St. Augustine to grow as fast as it possibly can. And those kinds of things are in the realm of either observational or experimental science. But the kind of science that we're talking about now is not just *forensic*, but it's *philosophical*.

Now, forensic science—if you like forensic kinds of shows like *Crime Scene Investigators*—what do they do? There's a crime. There's been a crime. And so the crime scene investigators go into the crime scene and do what? They look for evidence. They're looking for evidence that would tell them what happened and who did it. That's the drama in the TV shows, right? *Who did it?* Sometimes *how* they did it—because everybody's trying to figure out how to commit the perfect crime. The problem that we're running into with that is that the evidence is going to be very limited. And the further we are away from the event, the less the evidence is going to be, the more it's going to be degraded. And the more likely we are to be collecting evidence that may have nothing to do with what actually happened. There's something called *contamination*, right? Especially if it's an outdoor crime scene, it's very quickly and easily contaminated. So you're collecting evidence, it's scientific, but does that evidence connect to the event or not? You end up with *spurious* evidence and you're having to try to filter through what is the evidence of the *event* and what is evidence that may have come along *afterwards*. We run into those kinds of things with forensic science. It's not nearly an exact science. It's highly speculative, in fact.

Why Creation? Because of What it Reveals About God

And what could be more speculative than sitting here—if the universe is 15 billion years old—and speculating about what happened 15 billion years ago that got it this way or that got it started? It's pretty sketchy. And I go through that to illustrate to you that that is not really *science*. That's making up a story. This is what we *think* happened. And you can say, this is what I *think* happened. That's not necessarily what happened. It may have no connection at all to what happened. The creation account that Bill read a little while ago from the first chapter of Genesis describes a very orderly creation. God was very orderly and systematic in how he did things. And yes, it says he created in *six days*. Why is that so difficult to understand? Especially when you add in the fact that one of his reasons for creating light on the very first day was to mark the passage of the days—*morning and evening the first day, morning and evening the second day*—until we had the sun on day four that took the place of that original heavenly light. So it very clearly says that Genesis is a six-day event. And why should we doubt that if God is who we think he is based on what we said in that last session? We could put it this way. In the debate about how long it took God to create, scripture says it took six days. If he'd wanted to do it in an instant, he could have done it in an instant. As we saw, nothing's too hard for God. If he did it in six days, then there must be a *reason* why he did it in six days, and then that should drive us back to the scripture to understand what were God's intentions. What was he trying to teach from that process? So, no one was there at the beginning. No man was there. I can say that with confidence. Perhaps the angels were there observing creation, but man was not there to witness the creation. Man didn't come along until the very end, in fact.

Another thing that makes forensic science sketchy as a scientific method is that, unlike going out here and measuring how fast the grass is growing naturally or setting up an experiment in a laboratory, those things can be *repeated*. One-time events that are not *observed* and not *repeated*—that ends up being in a category besides science. And that's where things start to get sketchy. But when science tries to claim those kinds of things, that's where it's getting into trouble. And that's why we need to be able to differentiate between what constitutes good science, and the kind of science that is really operating according to an atheistic worldview and has an agenda behind it.

So we talked in the last session about how creation reveals who God is. We see him operating in a very orderly and a systematic way. Another thing that we see throughout the course of that week of creation, there is a certain refrain, there's more than one actually, that comes up. One of the refrains is, *and God said . . . and there was . . .* and then at the end of each of the days, what does he say as he looks over this creation—as it's beginning to take shape over the course of that first week? That it was *good . . .* that it was *good.* And that refrain continues until the end of the sixth day where he doesn't say, it is *good.* He says, it's *very good.* Now, how does that fit with the idea that over millions or billions of years, everything took place very slowly, randomly, that you had the formation of life, but you have lots of monsters that are fighting and killing each other and trying to survive until we finally end up with mankind? Doesn't quite fit the narrative. And we could not say, at any stage of that so-called process—if that's how it happened—that it was good. That would have been *bad.*

Science and Scripture

One of the things that fully convinced me some years ago about the necessity of six-day creation was a little book by Ken Ham called *Evolution: The Lie*. And I read that book and I thought, oh, well, yeah. Because his argument is that evolution depends on competition and death over millions and millions and millions and millions of years. But death did not enter the world until *what?* After the Fall. Everything was created very good. It was a perfect world. That has very important theological consequences, by the way. Everything was very good at the beginning, so there could not have been any death. There could not have been competition. We were not killing each other. Whether we were monkeys, or whatever we were on the way to becoming people, reptiles or whatever, right? The idea of evolution is a very violent and disorderly process, and that doesn't bear any resemblance to what God reveals in Genesis chapter 1.

So really it comes down to this question. Put science next to scripture and the question is: which one has authority over the other one? If science says this is how you have to interpret Genesis, then it didn't happen the way God said in Genesis chapter 1. It was evolution and billions of years and the word of God says *no*, it was six days, it was all very orderly and the end of it was all very good. *Which one of those has authority over the other?* Because one of them—here's the law of non-contradiction—one of them is wrong. And if we take science as the authority, which I don't recommend, by the way, then we have to rewrite scripture. Suddenly science—and this is a couple thousand years down the line in church history—suddenly science is the new hermeneutic. For several thousand years that God has been revealing himself through his Word, we didn't know how to interpret it until we got to science in the 20th century, that said, *here's how it really happened.* That's impossible. So keep in mind what's happening. And it's alarming to me again that so many Christians—well-known teachers and pastors—will simply refuse to defend Genesis chapter 1. They're willing to compromise and they may not realize just how severe the problem is.

No Common Ground

There's no common ground, particularly, between creation—biblical creation—and what passes for cosmology today, what's called the Big Bang. Now, there was some excitement in the middle of the 20th century when the Big Bang theory started getting bandied around, and scientists were a little uneasy with that because they're saying, *uh-oh, instead of an eternal universe, now we're talking about the universe having a beginning. That sounds a lot like Genesis.* And Christians may have been getting excited saying, *aha, science is finally showing that there was a beginning.*

But they're still not compatible. The new cosmology is not any more compatible with scripture than the last one. And just wait a while, a few generations maybe, who knows, the paradigm is going to change again. That's the nature of science. The story in science is always contingent. As I say, every conclusion is contingent upon the next observation.[33] I may go out there and make some conclusions about how the grass grows, and then tomorrow something happens, and I say, *oh, well, that was wrong*. I need a new theory, a new paradigm, because my data no longer fits. That's the nature of science. It never knows everything, and it never knows what it doesn't know. That's a really big problem.

We talk about the advances of science, for example, but compared to *what*? If we look at where we are today versus where we were 50 years ago, we say, *wow, look at these advances in science*. But if we'd been living 50 years ago, and some of us have—you might remember—before we knew all the things that we know today, we still thought we were pretty smart. Because we look back another 50 years and say, *well, look at how much we know today compared to what we knew 50 years ago*. But that pattern continues. Fifty years from now, it's going to be the same thing,

---

[33] The James Webb Space Telescope (JWST)—launched in December 2021 (a few months after this conference)—is proving the truth of this statement. Cosmologists are probing the edges of the visible universe, and guess what? They are not finding what they *expected* to find according to the Big Bang theory of cosmology.

and 100, and so forth. The proclamations of science, the ideas, the theories that it promotes are always changing. And the reason is because we're always *learning*. That's the process. We learn. We test. We keep what appears to make sense. And we reject it if it doesn't, and come up with new ideas. I've used the expression that the progress of science can be measured by the pile of discarded ideas out behind the laboratory. That's how science progresses. We take today's idea, we throw it on the trash heap, and we've got a new one to work with. And then a few days or a few years later, that one goes in the trash heap and here comes the next one. It's a very slow process.

The Idol of Wood

I'd like to turn your attention to a passage of scripture in the book of Jeremiah that recently came to my attention and seemed like a very fitting few verses to include in our discussion today. It fits in with what we've already been saying in the earlier sessions about the folly of idolatry. I'm in the 10th chapter of Jeremiah. And I would like to read the first ten verses. And by the way, this just adds to the point. This passage is an indictment against Israel—Israel's idolatry. They're on their way to judgment, or at least, we might say the *discipline* of being sent into exile. And what is it that's the recurring theme throughout the prophets? *Idolatry, idolatry, idolatry, idolatry*. Even if we're not paying very close attention, we might start to notice a pattern.

So, Jeremiah 10, starting in the first verse.

> Hear the word that the LORD speaks to you, O house of Israel. Thus says the LORD:
>
> "Learn not the way of the nations,
> >   nor be dismayed at the signs of the heavens
> >   because the nations are dismayed at them,
> for the customs of the peoples are vanity.
> A tree from the forest is cut down
> >   and worked with an axe by the hands of a craftsman.
> They decorate it with silver and gold;
> >   they fasten it with hammer and nails
> >   so that it cannot move.
> Their idols are like scarecrows in a cucumber field,
> >   and they cannot speak;
> they have to be carried,
> >   for they cannot walk.
> Do not be afraid of them,
> >   for they cannot do evil,
> >   neither is it in them to do good."
>
> There is none like you, O LORD;
> >   you are great, and your name is great in might.
> Who would not fear you, O King of the nations?
> >   For this is your due;
> for among all the wise ones of the nations
> >   and in all their kingdoms
> >   there is none like you.
> They are both stupid and foolish;

> the instruction of idols is but wood!
> Beaten silver is brought from Tarshish,
> > and gold from Uphaz.
> They are the work of the craftsman and of the hands of the goldsmith;
> > their clothing is violet and purple;
> > they are all the work of skilled men.
> But the LORD is the true God;
> > he is the living God and the everlasting King.
> At his wrath the earth quakes,
> > and the nations cannot endure his indignation.[34]

Now, I want to make an association. I want you to remember this passage. Maybe come back and read it a couple more times just to reinforce it, and then here's the association I want to create with you that I hope you never forget. *Evolution is an idol of wood.* It doesn't *speak*, can't *talk*, it has no *power*. As a so-called theory, it has no explanatory power. It doesn't explain anything. It's a *lie*, just as it says in the title of Ken Ham's book. Evolution is a lie. And more specifically, it's an *idol*. *It is a false religious system*, and it is in no way compatible with the revelation of scripture. Anything that we do—I could refer back to the passage from Psalm 115 that we looked at a few minutes ago, where the psalmist says, *not to us, O Lord, but to your name be the glory*—when we start introducing these idols of wood, we are taking glory away from the one who created the heavens and the earth and created it all very good. So don't let that happen in your mind and in your heart.

---

[34] Jer 10:1-10 (ESV).

Man on the Escalator

I propose this thought—that man is on the escalator. Here's a mental picture for you. Man on the escalator. If you see a snapshot—not a moving picture—man on the escalator is about halfway up. The question is, *is he going up or going down?* Because the two worldviews that we're talking about have two very different answers to that question. What does evolution say? Man is on the escalator *going up, getting better by the day.* What does the Bible say? Man was at the top, and he basically wrecked it. *He's on the way down.* And if there's any doubt about that, all you have to do is look around and see what's happening in the culture, and you can begin to grasp that.

Here's a little anecdote that I find fascinating, that if you look at surveys that ask people, *do you think things are getting better or worse?*—interestingly, they say, in a majority, *things are getting worse.* And the question is, *how would you know that?* You see, we already have the sense that things are getting worse, and the reason we know we're going down is because we still have the law written in our hearts, even though we're fallen.

Evolution says man is on the way up, and that opens the doors for all kinds all kinds of cruel and disgusting things. What do I mean by that?

We could talk about the Nazi Holocaust—of Hitler thinking that he was improving the stock of the race by eliminating the Jews. But the eugenics movement actually started in America.[35] And eugenics is a byproduct of an evolutionary worldview that says we're getting better as time goes by, and since we know that, we can do some things to help move the process along, speed it up a little. It is evil because it devalues human life. So the consequences are profound, and we see those consequences all around us in the culture and the way that we dehumanize life in so many ways.

A Miracle by any Definition

Now when we get to the bottom of it, we have to say that no matter what your worldview is, that the answer to the question how things got started is still a miracle. It doesn't matter what your worldview is. You can take the religion of atheism or you can take a Christian worldview—and frankly, as miracles go, I'm thinking a miracle that has God behind it probably makes more sense than a miracle that has absolutely nothing behind it. That really *is* a miracle if everything created itself out of nothing. That's a bigger miracle than even God could accomplish.

---

[35] Francis Galton coined the term "eugenics" in 1883. The resulting movement became more popular in early 20th century America than it had been in England.

So we need to understand the categories. The categories are not *science versus the Bible*, or *faith versus science*. It's not thinking about it correctly. That's actually—I would say this is part of Satan's deception—trying to get you to think that this is *science versus the Bible*. It's not. It's two competing worldviews that are in conflict.

Inconvenient Scientific Facts, and the Fallacy of Consensus

Now, I couldn't say much about science without talking about *the fallacy of consensus*. What is the fallacy of consensus? What is this story that you hear if we go back to climate change as an example of that? I posted something on Facebook recently about that, where one scientist declared, *we're now at more than a 99% consensus on man-made climate change, and there's no reason to have any more public discussion about this*. Huh. That's not the kind of science I was trained in. The kind of science I was trained in requires *reproducibility*. It requires the theory to fit the facts. Not, *here's an idea, and we're going to say it's true because we all believe it*. Is that science or is that faith? Because it's not hard to get a consensus. You know pollsters do that all the time, right? Every one of the polls that you see in the news, well, *51% of somebody believes this*. Well, it has a lot to do with the way you ask the question, and it has a lot to do with who you ask. And if you ask the right people the right question, guess what? Wow—consensus. It shouldn't be surprising, though, that in a world that now denies the objectivity of truth, that we're falling back on something called *consensus*. What else do we have? If there's no such thing as truth—if it's not a question of what is true or false—then it becomes a question of what do we mostly agree on. And that becomes the basis for what we do. So that idea of a consensus in science is, frankly, meaningless.

I'll give you just a quick anecdote of Albert Einstein, who, at the time that he came up with the Theory of Relativity, was not really part of the physics community, and yet he turned the physics community upside down. Newtonian physics had stood for several hundred years, and then it fell when Einstein came along. How many people does it take to overturn a theory, even if it's been around for generations? *Just one*. Because it's a question of the *truth*, not a question of what everybody agrees on.

As we get to the close of this session . . . well, before I do that, let me do one more thing. I did want to share with you a few examples of how science actually agrees with scripture. It might shock you for me to say that science actually agrees with scripture. Well, it does. What do we mean by that? Think back to what Bill was reading at the beginning of this session. Here is one of the refrains from that first chapter of Genesis. *After its kind . . . after its kind*. What is the law that God built into the creatures? Everything reproduces *after its own kind*. That alone makes evolution impossible. You cannot have a flamingo that turns into a giraffe. Flamingos make flamingos, giraffes make giraffes, and that's always true. And if you want an illustration of how we've tried to overturn that law, you can look at the research that's been done in the area of using fruit flies because they reproduce very quickly. We've been trying to make fruit flies into something else for the last 100 years. And a funny thing happens. Fruit flies only produce fruit flies. And another funny thing happens. The ones that are mutated often don't reproduce anything. Everything reproduces after its own kind. There's a scientific fact for you. Does that preclude variation within species? No. In fact, I noticed as I'm looking around the room, nobody in this room looks exactly alike. And if we had twice or three times as many people, that would still be true. Nobody's going to look exactly alike. And it's actually remarkable—and points back to God in his original creation of Adam and Eve—that all the variation of all the people in all the world that would ever be born was already in the genes of Adam when he was created. You're not a *mutation*. You're a *variation* of what God originally created.

Another one—this one hits hard as far as our culture goes right at the moment—that it says in verse 27, *God created man in his own image, in the image of God he created him.* Well, it's hard for me to say this. *Male and female, he created them*. There is *male* and there is *female*, according to God's creation, according to his original design. That may not be true in every species, but it's true in most. We see, for example—if we skip ahead a few chapters to Genesis 6, as Noah is preparing the ark for the Flood—what happens? God brings the animals to Noah in pairs, *male and female*, so that they can reproduce after the Flood. It's been that way from the beginning and it's that way from now on. It's not going to change. Our efforts to try to change the nature of gender—or to deny it—are fruitless. And it's unfortunate that we will take something that ought to be a good thing—which is medical science—and use it for self-mutilation and to try to be something that we are not. It's a violent denial of the nature that God made us to reflect.

Another important consequence—we'll talk a little more about this in the next section—is that when it says *God made man in his own image* and *made man male and female*, that an important consequence of that is, whether you're male or female, that you have the capacity to fully reflect God's image. So whatever God's image is, at the end of the day, whether you're male or female, you can perfectly reflect that image, because Eve did. Both Adam and Eve did. It was not simply *man*, as in Adam, made in God's image, but man made in God's image, *male and female*. And yet we can see that male and female are different from each other. I know a president of Harvard got himself fired for saying that in public. It's not politically correct to say that.

It's also the case—and this is another thing that we have to be cautious of with regard to evolution—is that *people and animals are categorically different*. When we start talking about what does it mean to be made in the image of God, Lisa's cats are not made in the image of God. Your dog Fido is not made in the image of God. *You* are—and that makes you unique.

Another important consideration that scripture gives us is that *there's only one human race*. Every human being who has ever lived has descended from Adam and Eve. And all this stuff about *race* that we talk about, because we don't all have the same skin tone—imagine that, God has made varieties—but there's only one human race. And so when I was saying at the outset that part of the reason for Genesis is that it helps us answer virtually all the issues that we're wrestling with today, that's an example of what I mean.

Now as we get ready for our lunch break, let me close this session with a quote from John MacArthur:

> If we cannot believe what Genesis says about origins, we are lost as to our purpose and our destiny. Whether this world and

its life as we know it evolved by chance, without a cause, or was created by God, has immense comprehensive implications for all human life.

Amen.

Session 4: Man Made in God's Image

Scripture (Gen 1:26-28)

> Then God said, "Let us make man in our image, after our likeness. And let them have dominion over the fish of the sea and over the birds of the heavens and over the livestock and over all the earth and over every creeping thing that creeps on the earth."
>
> So God created man in his own image,
> > in the image of God he created him;
> > male and female he created them.
>
> And God blessed them. And God said to them, "Be fruitful and multiply and fill the earth and subdue it, and have dominion over the fish of the sea and over the birds of the heavens and over every living thing that moves on the earth."[36]

Introduction

So we're moving on to session 4 now, where we begin to talk about what it means to be made in the image of God. There's obviously something unique about this. There's nothing else in creation that's described in this particular way. And scripture doesn't always give us a clear picture of what that means. But I'll pick up on something that Kirk just prayed for, and that is the idea that as Christians, in our sanctification, what

---

[36] Gen 1:26-28 (ESV).

we have *lost* in the Fall, we are *regaining* in our sanctification—that *we are being remade into the image of Christ*. And who then is that perfect image? And that is Jesus himself. And it says that *we do not yet know what we will be, but when we see him, we will be like him*. So there's that idea that whatever is captured in the essence of what it means to be fully human that we see in Christ what our sanctification is about. But first, how did we get to the situation we're in now?

I'm going to start again—I referred earlier to a TV show called *CSI* that I used to watch some years ago, *Crime Scene Investigation*. And the original version of that, for its theme song, used a popular song called "Who Are You?" And that's the question that we're trying to ask at this point. When Kirk says, *why am I here? What's happening to me? Why is this happening to me?* It's really part of the question of who are you and understanding who you are. What does the world have to say about that? Well, the world says you're *nothing*. But the Bible has a different, a much different view of that. And so this question of who we are—not just a question of what my name is or where I live or where I went to school and those kinds of identifying things—but *what we are as man*. That's what we're interested in knowing a little better.

Now, in one of the books that I've read by Schaeffer, he talks about his experience at L'Abri in Switzerland. And what must be a very frustrating thing for anybody in ministry, someone comes to you in a state of despair. They have been listening to everything that the world has to say about them basically being evolved germs—grown-up germs emerging from the slime—that their lives really don't have any meaning, that whatever pain they may be feeling or whatever thing they may be suffering is meaningless, it has no purpose. And in what must have been kind of a brilliant pastoral moment, Schaeffer could look at the one who is despairing of what the world has to offer to the answer to the question, *who are you?* and say, *I know who you are.* I know who you are. Because he knows who that person is—made in the image of God. Maybe that's something that Kirk can use in some of his patient counseling. So that's the question that we come to. Who are we? And what does this mean specifically for us to be made in the image of God?

I want to borrow once more from what the Westminster Divines set down for us in the *Westminster Confession*, and this time in chapter 4, paragraph 2. And there we read:

> After God had made all other creatures, he created man, male and female, with reasonable and immortal souls, endued with knowledge, righteousness, and true holiness, after his own image . . .

And there's an important beginning for us to understand what it means to be made in his image.

> . . . *reasonable and immortal souls, endued with knowledge, righteousness, and true holiness, after his own image,* having the law of God written in their hearts, and power to fulfil it; and yet under a possibility of transgressing, being left to the liberty of their own will, which was subject unto change. Beside this law written in their hearts, they received a command not to eat of the tree of the knowledge of good and evil; which while they kept they were happy in their communion with God, and had dominion over the creatures.[37]

So as we start to look at this, we have to keep in mind that when we come to the next session and talk about the Fall and the effects of the Fall, it might be tempting to think that the Fall erased the image of God in man. But it must not have done that. There is still a remnant of that image left. We have an important clue to that found in Genesis 9 after the Flood when God gives the command to Noah that *whosoever sheds the blood of man, by man his blood will be shed*—and the reason appended to that is that man is made in the image of God. So that image is still there. It's certainly damaged. It's not what it was originally. And it's not yet what it will be, but that essential aspect of that image of God is still there.

---

[37] *Westminster Confession of Faith*, Chapter 4.2.

Science Says: We are the Sum of Our Parts

Now, Kirk works in a field that in many ways is very secular, very scientific, very analytical. And we could ask, *what does science have to say about what it means to be human?* And it generally comes down to this, that you're just the sum of your parts: your atoms, your molecules, your systems, everything working together, what we might call a fortuitous arrangement, of course, all as a product of evolution taking place very slowly over millions and millions of years. Of course, anyone who's studied the anatomy of the body or even the anatomy of the cell is completely stunned by the complexity and the order that's found there. It's not possible that it could have happened by chance. And yet, that's the dominant view. Without God, what are we? We're a collection of molecules.

Now, interestingly, the medical profession is designed to help do things like alleviate suffering and to cure disease, to repair the body when it's broken, and to help it to heal. But more and more, what do we see? Kirk referred to *euthanasia*. And there's an oxymoron, if there ever was one, because euthanasia literally means *good death*. Euthanasia—as we use the term—is murder. Taking the life of someone, even near death. And that's forbidden. There's no biblical justification for that at all. But that drives us to ask the question, again, as Kirk raised the question, *why am*

I suffering? If it's wrong to end suffering by taking the life of someone, even near the end of his life, then there must be a reason for suffering. But in the secular world, we can't make sense out of those kinds of things. The secular world will look at suffering and say, *oh, suffering is bad, period, we have to stop it*. If we can alleviate it with medication, we'll do that. But if necessary, we'll stop the suffering by ending a life. And that's wrong.

So in the world of science, you're just the sum of your parts. Schaeffer has an interesting way of putting this worldview. He calls it *the material-energy, chance view of reality*. The material-energy, chance view of reality. Everything is the way it is purely by chance. The idea of materialism is that we're just stuff. Whatever we are, we're just composed of stuff. The world is composed of stuff and we are just the sum of our stuff, whatever it happens to be. And trying to assign some value to it, trying to assign some meaning to it, is a fruitless effort because everything is just stuff at the end of the day.

Humanism Says: We are Bodies Without Souls

Now the Enlightenment brought us this idea—and it turned out to be a futile one—so the Enlightenment didn't go very far philosophically—it attempted to understand truth using reason without a knowledge of

God. Remember what we were saying at the beginning—that even Adam and Eve in their state of perfection needed God's word to know what was right and wrong and to be able to discern. Rationalism says, *we're just going to use our minds*. We're rational beings. We're going to think it through and we're going to figure it out on the basis of where our thoughts take us. So the rationalist looks around at the universe and says, *well, this seems to be a very ordered place*. Everything works in a very orderly kind of way and there seem to be these natural laws that govern how everything works. And so we see in cause-and-effect, if one thing happens, then the effect is something else on the basis of whatever the natural law is that governs that. And on the basis of that, if we keep going with our rationalism, we end up saying that the universe is a machine and man is just part of the machinery. And it's a pretty pessimistic view because it basically means that whatever we may think we have, in the way of free will or the ability to think for ourselves, is just an illusion. Because everything can be predicted if we know the antecedent events. Everything follows a very mechanistic view. And so that means that man is really nothing but a cog in the machinery. He may *think* he has free will, he may *think* he thinks for himself, but he really doesn't. And that brought us to a point of despair. That's as far as Enlightenment rationalism could get us. And if man is just a machine, then man isn't much. We have to draw the inevitable conclusion that we're just a product of the forces of the universe.

So that led us to Existentialism, or what Schaeffer calls *the upper story leap* into mysticism. Logic took us down the road of despair. If we wanted to get back some idea of meaning, then we were going to have to give up reason in order to get to it. That wasn't much of an improvement.

Now, the dominant philosophy of our time is called *humanism*. And we could say there are many shades of it. But it's the same kind of idea—starting with man and trying to reason from what we have without assuming the existence of God so that there's really no inherent *purpose* in our lives and, by the same degree, there is no inherent *value* to our lives. And as philosophy goes, that should scare you a little bit because that ends up leading us into a collectivist kind of view. And what I mean by that—one of the buzzwords that you'll hear that is a dog whistle—is when you start hearing people talking about, *well, this is for the common good*. Well, what does that mean? That means somebody is not going to turn out well. For one person to do well, somebody else is going to lose. And in a humanistic worldview, there is no argument against that. This is the kind of view that would say, *well, our hospitals are full of old patients who are dying. They're probably terminally ill. Let's just go ahead and put them down like an old mutt so that we can clear out the resources and allow younger people to have access to the resources.* It takes a very utilitarian view of human life.

There's something else in Schaeffer that is a very sticky idea, though. He talks about the *manishness of man* in his usual odd kind of way of speaking. And it's that idea that man knows that there's something that's different about man. There is something, as it were, written in the heart that tells him he is *different*, that his life is *not* meaningless, his life is *not* an accident, that there is something *unique* about it and something *valuable* about it. Humanism, however, as a worldview—and this is interesting if you read the Humanist Manifestos—that it says that *science has disproved the idea of a separable soul*. Somehow or another—and I was napping at the time—science managed to prove something that's metaphysical—the idea that man does *not* have a soul. And of course, we know from the biblical account that man *does* have a soul, and that is part of what makes him unique. He is both body and soul, or body and spirit. But humanism tries to deny the existence of the soul. And part of the consequence of that, if there is no soul, then when your life is over, it's *over*. There's nothing that continues beyond the grave. There's nothing beyond the grave for you to find. And certainly there is no one beyond the grave to hold you accountable.

Economics Says: You're Worth What You Produce

Another consequence of this kind of humanistic view is that we start engaging in an *economic* calculus. We say, *what is the value of a human life?* And I guarantee you—I don't know if Kirk has started to run into this or not—but I guarantee you this is coming. Oh, you're 80 years old. Well, we're not going to pay for you to have a knee replacement. Because why? Well, you're already at the end of your life. There's no reason for spending money on someone who's already near the end of his life. But if you're in too much pain, we'll give you some morphine, and you can take as much of that as you want.

So there's inevitably—when we go down this kind of road—a utilitarian way of thinking. We're going to be changing what it means to be human by the way that we try to place a value on human life. Biblically, how do we do that? What is the value of a human life from the standpoint of scripture? Well, here's one of those places where we run into a temporal limitation. And what I mean by that is, *how do you measure the value of a soul with something that's temporal or temporary, like money?* Is your soul worth a million dollars—or *two* million? What is the price of a soul? And we'll look at a verse in a moment that attempts to answer that question.

So we end up—if we go down that pathway—in what's called a *quality of life* ethic. And it maybe sounds reasonable on the surface, but it ought to scare you. Because it basically says, when you get to a certain age or you have a certain kind of illness or disability, that someone else is going to determine for you that the quality of your life is not worth saving—that the quality of your life is not worth living. So there's a profound difference—just as the difference between creation and evolution—between a *quality of life* ethic that is humanistic, where there's no intrinsic value to human life, and a *sanctity of life* ethic.

What was it that we were fighting for so many years ago when we started *Lufkin for Life?*[38] We could say, *well, we were fighting against Planned Parenthood*. That might be true enough. But what we were really doing in the process was articulating a sanctity of life ethic—that all life is precious, especially life in the womb from the moment of conception. It's not something for us to simply decide that if we don't *want* it or it's *inconvenient* that we discard it, or if we think that it's too *expensive*, as if we could measure the value of a human life with dollars and cents.

So in all those kinds of things, those humanistic views, we don't have a doctrine of suffering. And in fact, it's one of the common objections to Christianity. It goes something like this: *if God is good and God is all-powerful, then why does he allow suffering?* And the answer is, if God is good and God is all-powerful and he allows suffering, then *he must have a good reason for it*. And then he must be able to bring some good out of

---

[38] In 2004, this congregation helped to charter a prolife organization. I served as Director until we disbanded in 2008.

it. And that's what we need to understand. So suffering—even suffering in the Christian view—is not without meaning. It's not without purpose. It doesn't diminish the difficulty of it. The reality of it comes as a result of the Fall, which we'll talk about in the next session. But at least in a Christian worldview—we could say it this way—that our suffering is redeemed, that there is a purpose in it, and that suffering is not, as it were, a reason for rejecting Christianity. Because we wrongly assume that if God were good, he would stop it. At this point, it might be helpful to remember that it wasn't God who brought suffering and death into the world. That would be *us*. That was on *us*.

Incomparable Worth

So we talked a little bit before lunch about how, in the narrative of creation, as we read the unfolding narrative of six-day creation, it seems to be a story with a *direction*. It's going somewhere. And so it culminates then on that last day with the creation of Adam and Eve in the image of God. We could say that God was saving the best for last. And it's unfortunate—and this is part of the Fall—that even though we are given incredible dignity as creatures made in the image of God, that we seem to spend a lot of our time denigrating that and trying to tear it down. It's kind of like the idea of taking a beautiful painting and just spraying it with graffiti. We are besmirching what was made beautiful and valuable, infinitely valuable.

Now, one of the narratives that you hear, especially in regard to climate change, there's this inherent idea that somehow man is bad, and there are those who will even argue that man is literally a plague on the planet, and it might be better if he were mostly wiped out. I guess *mostly*, not including those who are saying that he should be wiped out. There are always going to be exceptions. But is man a plague? What is the purpose of this creation? God made the heavens and the earth, and he made it to be inhabited. He made it as the theater of redemption where this unfolding story of redemption would play out. This world is temporary. Our scientists may say it's been here for four and a half billion years, but based on the scriptural evidence, we wouldn't agree with that—it's only been here a few thousand years. And it may be here for a few thousand more, we don't know. But the idea that the Earth is still going to be here in five billion years, that's a guess. And that's not a justification for saying that what we are doing now—which is using the world's resources and supposedly destroying the planet—is a problem. If it's the case that the Lord returns tomorrow when we still have plenty of coal and oil and gas, then there was more than enough here for the time that we needed it. And we have to trust that God and his wisdom would provide the resources that we would need, whether in terms of food or energy or those kinds of things.

Let's look at Isaiah 45, verses 18 and 19. And here we have another reminder of God as the Creator:

> For thus says the LORD,
> who created the heavens
>   (he is God!),
> who formed the earth and made it
>   (he established it;
> he did not create it empty,
>   *he formed it to be inhabited!*):
> "I am the LORD, and there is no other.
> I did not speak in secret,
>   in a land of darkness;
> I did not say to the offspring of Jacob,
>   'Seek me in vain.'
> I the LORD speak the truth;
>   I declare what is right.[39]

So God intends for man to thrive upon the earth. What do we see in the very opening narrative of Genesis, in chapter 1?

For those who are lying awake at night worrying about population explosion, I've got to press the question, *where did you get that idea?*

---

[39] Is 45:18-19 (ESV).

Because you didn't get it from scripture. You may have gotten it from Malthus or, what's his name? Paul Erlich.

There are those who have predicted the end of the universe or the end of the earth because of overpopulation and yet the scripture is very clear from the beginning that God made life to *multiply*, to *reproduce*, to *fill the earth*. And that command was given to the *whole* earth, wasn't it?

Look at verse 22 in Genesis chapter 1, referring to the creatures:

> And God blessed them, saying, "Be fruitful and multiply and fill the waters in the seas, and let birds multiply on the earth."[40]

And he later gives the same command to man, and more than once. And in fact, if you remember a little further along in Genesis after the Flood, after God said, *I want you to disperse abroad over the whole earth*. And man said, *nah, here's a good spot, let's stay here*. And what resulted from that? God came down and confused the languages and scattered the families abroad so that they could not just stay in one place. We're meant to scatter abroad.

I was just noticing—I just happened to notice this on the way from Colorado down here to Texas and across a good portion of Texas—that

---

[40] Gen 1:22 (ESV).

there's still a lot of open space. I think there's still room for a few more people. And anybody who's flown across the country would probably say the same thing. There are vast expanses of this country—and every country—that are yet uninhabited. And yet, why do we fret so much about population control? Man is made in God's image, and God says to him, *be fruitful and multiply, fill the earth, and have dominion over it.* And yet man says, *I think we're wiser than that, and we're not going to do that.*

Imago Dei: The Breath of Life

Now let's take a look at Genesis 2 as we start to dial-in a little more this idea of the imago Dei. Take a look at verse 7 in chapter 2. It says:

> . . . then the LORD God formed the man of dust from the ground and breathed into his nostrils the breath of life, and the man became a living creature.[41]

Now here's something for us to think about for a moment. The first thing that God did was form Adam's body. If we had been there at that moment, we would have seen Adam. He might have looked like he was asleep, but he was still just dust, wasn't he? Like clay formed from the ground. And it wasn't until that moment when *God breathed into him*

---

[41] Gen 2:7 (ESV).

the breath of life that he became a living being. And what seems to be more unusual about this creation than the other parts of creation that we've seen so far? We notice that it's very *personal* and that it's God's breath himself that breathes into the man life. And this breath is referring to the *soul*, that man has a soul. And that makes him unique in all the creation, because nothing else that God has created so far has a soul. It may be material or flesh, but after it perishes, it's gone. It returns to the ground. But something's unique about man—that even though man's body may return to the ground after death, his soul returns to the Lord. So man has a soul that lives forever.

One of my former pastors used to like referring to man as *animated dust*. I'm trying to think of who that was. But the spirit of man lives on. God has made that spirit to live forever. And one of the reasons why we cannot simply try to value mankind on the basis of what he can *do* or what he *consists of* is that the most important thing that he consists of is metaphysical. What is the value of a man's soul? And we can't put a price on it.

This man also has particular responsibilities. He's given *dominion* over all the rest of creation. And he's also bounded by a *law*, and we see that a little further down in chapter 2. The *Confession* that we read from a little while ago referred to this. Verse 16:

> And the LORD God commanded the man, saying, "You may surely eat of every tree of the garden, but of the tree of the knowledge of good and evil you shall not eat, for in the day that you eat of it you shall surely die."[42]

So here God places man in the Garden, surrounds him with every kind of tree that's good for food, places no limitations at all on what he can eat or how much, or when, but then there's this *one* line in the sand, so to speak. There's this *one* tree that's off limits. And as we'll see, part of what's happening here is that while God is establishing Adam to have dominion over this creation, there's a limit to that dominion. He doesn't have dominion over all of it because there's a part of it that God has created that he says, *that part's not for you*. And that's going to represent the test that we see when we get to the next chapter. Is man going to stay within the bounds of the dominion that God has assigned to him, or is he going to be tempted to leave that proper bound?

This limitation has two parts as well. There's a limitation in terms of the *authority*. In other words, think of it as, you know, if you walk outside here, there's a fence around your property. That fence represents the boundary between your property and the next property, and it's not for you to cross that fence into someone else's property. In the same way, God says, *I'm putting a fence around this tree, that one's*

---

[42] Gen 2:16-17 (ESV).

mine, all the rest are yours. Is Adam going to fall into the temptation of crossing that boundary, of taking some property that's not his? And the other thing that that tree represents, as we'll see, is *knowledge*.

So we see that as Adam is created, even in his perfection, he is limited both in terms of authority and in terms of knowledge, and that his temptation is going to be to grasp something that's outside of his authority and to reach for knowledge that God has not intended for him to have. Does God intend for his creatures to have complete knowledge? The answer is, of course not. We are finite creatures. Even if we wanted to, we couldn't have omniscience. But it is the case that God has revealed to us what he *wants* us to know and what we *need* to know, and therein we're supposed to be content.

There's a verse that captures that idea. Pretty familiar verse in Deuteronomy:

> "The secret things belong to the LORD our God, but the things that are revealed belong to us and to our children forever . . ."

And it doesn't stop there. It also goes on to say:

> ". . . *that we may do all the words of this law.*"[43]

---

[43] Deut 29:29 (ESV).

So God intends for us to know his law and to live according to his law, to live within the bounds of that law, to live with the knowledge that he has given to us, and not to grasp after those things that he has set off limits to us. So man is reminded, as it were, in the creation, even though he's given dominion, that his dominion necessarily has limits because he as a creature has limits.

One Man Adam, One Human Race

As we mentioned in the last session, one of the important consequences of the creation account of Adam as the first man and Eve as the first woman is that all people everywhere are descended from them. Many varieties, many colors, many different languages, but all one human race so that the idea that we can arbitrarily divide people into different races, that's problematical from the very beginning. We may have different backgrounds, but we are nevertheless one race.

We also talked some about the fact that God makes man male and female. And when we look at the anarchy of our present age and the insanity of it, the idea that if we go back, let's say, 50 years to the 60s, the big deal was sexual anarchy. *I don't want to be restrained at all.* And then that turned into homosexuality. And now what do we have? We have this movement that says, *well, I'm not male or female, I'm whatever*

I want to be, and even if I was made one or the other, I can deny that and try to be something else and use every means possible to do that whether chemical or surgical. And how much of a repudiation is that of the manner in which God has made us? He's made us male and female by his *design* and for his *purpose*. And it's as if man is trying to distance himself as much as he can from God as God originally created him. And it's an act of futility.

Bringing Life from the Dust

As we start to bring this session to a close, I want to take a look at John chapter 11. We have the story in Genesis 1 that we just looked at—how God formed Adam out of the dust and breathed into him the breath of life. Again, that's nothing less than a miracle. There is no natural process by which something that's non-living can become living. I'll give you an anecdote that I recently saw that helps illustrate the point. And that's the idea that when you buy a jug of milk and it says on the milk that it's *pasteurized*, it's *de facto* proof that life doesn't come from non-life. The whole point of pasteurizing a jug of milk is that it's not going to grow bacteria because bacteria don't grow unless there's already bacteria there to grow. But if you kill what's living, then nothing else grows because *life does not come from non-life.*

I can illustrate in a little more graphic way what I call *the frog in the blender*. Go take a frog and put him in a blender, put it on puree for twenty or thirty seconds, turn the blender off, remove the lid, and wait for the frog to come out. And you say, *well, the frog's not coming back out*. And my response is, *why not?* All the ingredients for life are in the blender. Everything that's necessary for life is already in the blender. I'm giving you a big head start. But we know that life does not come from non-life, not without the intervention of the Creator.

And so we come to John 11. This is the narrative of the raising of Lazarus. Let me start in verse 17 to capture more of the narrative here:

> Now when Jesus came, he found that Lazarus had already been in the tomb four days. Bethany was near Jerusalem, about two miles off, and many of the Jews had come to Martha and Mary to console them concerning their brother. So when Martha heard that Jesus was coming, she went and met him, but Mary remained seated in the house. Martha said to Jesus, "Lord, if you had been here, my brother would not have died. But even now I know that whatever you ask from God, God will give you." Jesus said to her, "Your brother will rise again." Martha said to him, "I know that he will rise again in the resurrection on the last day." Jesus said to her, "I am the resurrection and the life. Whoever believes in me, though he die, yet shall he live, and everyone who lives and believes in me shall never die. Do you believe this?" She said to him, "Yes, Lord; I believe that you are the Christ, the Son of God, who is coming into the world."

When she had said this, she went and called her sister Mary, saying in private, "The Teacher is here and is calling for you." And when she heard it, she rose quickly and went to him. Now Jesus had not yet come into the village, but was still in the place where Martha had met him. When the Jews who were with her in the house, consoling her, saw Mary rise quickly and go out, they followed her, supposing that she was going to the tomb to weep there. Now when Mary came to where Jesus was and saw him, she fell at his feet, saying to him, "Lord, if you had been here, my brother would not have died." When Jesus saw her weeping, and the Jews who had come with her also weeping, he was deeply moved in his spirit and greatly troubled. And he said, "Where have you laid him?" They said to him, "Lord, come and see." Jesus wept. So the Jews said, "See how he loved him!" But some of them said, "Could not he who opened the eyes of the blind man also have kept this man from dying?"

Then Jesus, deeply moved again, came to the tomb. It was a cave, and a stone lay against it. Jesus said, "Take away the stone." Martha, the sister of the dead man, said to him, "Lord, by this time there will be an odor, for he has been dead four days." Jesus said to her, "Did I not tell you that if you believed you would see the glory of God?" So they took away the stone. And Jesus lifted up his eyes and said, "Father, I thank you that you have heard me. I knew that you always hear me, but I said this on account of the people standing around, that they may believe that you sent me." When he had said these things, he cried out with a loud voice, "Lazarus, come out." The man who had died came out, his hands and feet bound with linen strips, and his face wrapped with a cloth. Jesus said to them, "Unbind him, and let him go."[44]

---

[44] John 11:17-44 (ESV).

This is even more remarkable than my disgusting analogy of the frog in the blender because someone who's been dead for four days is going to have more than an odor. Decomposition by this time has set in considerably. And yet, this one who calls to life the dead is also the one that we read earlier who created in the beginning, created all things, and sustains all things. Science doesn't explain these kinds of things. Science says that can't happen. That sort of thing doesn't happen. It's interesting that they would deny the resurrection, saying that it couldn't happen, when they're the ones who are telling us that life came out of non-life in the beginning. And it kept evolving and becoming more complex, completely on its own, without any directed effort. And there's part of the inconsistency of an unbelieving worldview. We can't make sense out of what we're seeing.

Now this is an important story for more than one reason. Obviously, Jesus raising Lazarus from the dead is a picture of Jesus raising all the dead on the last day. It's also a picture that connects us back to creation, the one who breathes the breath of life into the dust of Adam and makes him a living being. And part of what is being expressed here when Jesus says, *I am*, takes us back. And let's look at Exodus 3. This is where Moses is in the wilderness and sees the burning bush and turns aside to see what this is about. And he begins this conversation with God, where God tells him he's going to be sent to lead the people of

Israel out of their captivity in Egypt. And I'll pick up the narrative in verse 13 of chapter 3.

> Then Moses said to God, "If I come to the people of Israel and say to them, 'The God of your fathers has sent me to you,' and they ask me, 'What is his name?' what shall I say to them?" God said to Moses, "I AM WHO I AM." And he said, "Say this to the people of Israel: 'I AM has sent me to you.'"[45]

When Jesus starts using these expressions, *I AM the resurrection and the life, I AM the way and the truth and the life, I AM the door to the sheepfold, I AM the good shepherd* and so forth, he's making statements of *deity*. He is more than just a teacher. He is a Savior and he is the one who has created us and the one who has the power of resurrection, the power of life in himself. And we would all do well to heed the call that he makes for those to put their trust in him for salvation because there is salvation in no other.

We'll close this session by considering a short quotation from Louis Berkhof, where he says:

> The doctrine of the image of God in man is of the greatest importance in theology, for that image is the expression of that which is most distinctive in man and in his relation to God.[46]

---

[45] Ex 3:13-14 (ESV).
[46] *Systematic Theology*, Banner of Truth Trust, 1958, p. 206.

Man has infinite worth because he is created in God's image. And it is precisely the work that Christ is doing in the renewal of that fallen spirit to bring man back into the image and likeness that God created him with.

Amen.

Session 5: Creation Ruined

Scripture (Gen 3:1-7)

> Now the serpent was more crafty than any other beast of the field that the LORD God had made. He said to the woman, "Did God actually say, 'You shall not eat of any tree in the garden'?" And the woman said to the serpent, "We may eat of the fruit of the trees in the garden, but God said, 'You shall not eat of the fruit of the tree that is in the midst of the garden, neither shall you touch it, lest you die.'" But the serpent said to the woman, "You will not surely die. For God knows that when you eat of it your eyes will be opened, and you will be like God, knowing good and evil." So when the woman saw that the tree was good for food, and that it was a delight to the eyes, and that the tree was to be desired to make one wise, she took of its fruit and ate, and she also gave some to her husband who was with her, and he ate. Then the eyes of both were opened, and they knew that they were naked. And they sewed fig leaves together and made themselves loincloths.[47]

Introduction

There's a particular radio program that I listen to on a regular basis called *The White Horse Inn*. Many of you may be familiar with it. And one of the interesting things that they often do on *The White Horse Inn* is that the producer—a man named Shane Rosenthal—will go from place to place doing man-on-the-street interviews. Sometimes it'll be at

---

[47] Gen 3:1-7 (ESV).

a college campus, sometimes it'll be at a Christian bookseller's convention, different places like that, sometimes just men on the street, so to speak. And when you hear these kind of interviews, and people are asked the question about the nature of man, they inevitably answer in the affirmative if they're asked, *is man basically good or bad?* What's their answer? Well, of course, *man is basically good*. And that is arguably one of the most persistent myths, not just in the Christian world, but in the whole world, period. Man is in a state of denial about his own condition, thinking himself to be good. And of course, if you lower the bar far enough, you can make yourself good. Of course. But this is also a myth that has also plagued the church over the years. It shows up at various times in various different forms. You may have heard of something called *Pelagianism*. That was an early controversy during the first millennium of the church. And Pelagius was attempting to argue that man's condition is the same now as it was before the Fall. That there is no bias, as it were, towards sin. And his teaching was condemned as a heresy, as it well should be. Scripture is quite clear that man's condition is not just damaged, but ruined. And of course, later on you have the controversy with the Arminians who are trying to argue something similar, perhaps to a lesser degree. Yes, man has been affected by the Fall, but not so completely damaged by the Fall that he doesn't have some good motion left in his will. The question is whether that lines up at all with what scripture says, and the answer is, well, as a matter of fact, *no*, it doesn't.

In fact, we don't have to look any further than a couple of short verses in Genesis 6, where God gives, as it were, the judgment against the earth at that time. If you want, we'll go ahead and look at that. Now that I've referred to it, we have to look at it, don't we? Where in verse 5 he says:

> The LORD saw that the wickedness of man was great in the earth, and that every intention of the thoughts of his heart was only evil continually.[48]

And in verse 11:

> Now the earth was corrupt in God's sight, and the earth was filled with violence. And God saw the earth, and behold, it was corrupt, for all flesh had corrupted their way on the earth.[49]

And if you follow the general flow of Genesis, from chapter 3 down to chapter 6, what you seem to be seeing is this downward progression that we were talking about earlier. This is the down escalator. The Fall was bad. The Fall brought sin. It brought the Curse. But things weren't as

---

[48] Gen 6:5 (ESV).
[49] Gen 6:11-12 (ESV).

bad as they were going to get over the succeeding generations. And so as we go from chapter 3—where the Fall of Adam and Eve occurs—to chapter 4, we find that the first man who was conceived in sin and born into this fallen world grows up to become the world's first murderer. And then it only gets worse from there. At least, it seems that Cain had some pangs of conscience. He was concerned that someone might try to avenge Abel's murder. But a few generations later, in Cain's line, his offspring, there's a man named Lamech. We're told in verse 19, Lamech took two wives. One was Adah and the name of the other was Zillah. We see the perversion of marriage into polygamy by this time. Then we're told about his sons and what they did. But let's jump down to verse 23.

> Lamech said to his wives:
>
> "Adah and Zillah, hear my voice;
>   you wives of Lamech, listen to what I say:
> I have killed a man for wounding me,
>   a young man for striking me.
> If Cain's revenge is sevenfold,
>   then Lamech's is seventy-sevenfold."[50]

Now what that's referring to is when Cain is banished, what's one of his complaints against God? *Well, somebody's going to find me and kill me.* And God says, *no, I'm going to put a mark on you. I'm not going to permit*

---

[50] Gen 4:23-24 (ESV).

your murder to be avenged. And if anyone takes your life, I'm going to avenge him seven times. Lamech says, *I can do better than that.* You see the hardness of the heart of this man who seems to have no pangs of conscience at all about murder by this time. We see, as it were, in a shadowy form, the descent of man into greater and greater violence and corruption until we get to this judgment that God pronounces at the beginning of Genesis 6 that *the wickedness of man was great in the earth and that every intention of the thoughts of his heart was only evil continually* and that *the earth was corrupt and filled with violence.*

We might notice that the normal kind of civil restraints against violence were not present in this pre-Flood time. It wasn't until Genesis chapter 9, after the Flood, when the death penalty for murder is first instituted. What happens in a world where there are few consequences for crime or for sin? And the answer is, it simply multiplies, doesn't it? We don't have to look very hard at what's been happening in our own culture over these last couple of years to see that when we start denigrating our police, or we start getting rid of them, we start making it impossible for them to do their jobs, we start making approval of violence and theft, then guess what? We're going to get more crime and more violence. This is the nature of man and that's why God imposes an assortment of restraints on man.

"Man is Great, But he is Cruel"

We talked about one of those restraints just a little while ago. What was going to happen if Nimrod was left in the plain of Shinar to build his city and to build his tower—where all mankind was gathered together at one place and one time? It was going to be the multiplication of sin once again. So by scattering people, God helps diffuse the effects of sin. So there are an assortment of ways that we see through scripture how God deals with sin and helps to mitigate the effects so that it's not as bad as it could be. But it's inevitable that when those restraints start to fall away—whether it's *individual* restraints, restraints within the *family*, restraints within *civil society*—that the result is more and more corruption, more violence.

This is the condition of man, and the irony is that man somehow continues to insist that he's basically good. Talk about denial! Schaeffer puts it this way, he says, *man is great, but he is cruel*. Now there's quite a dichotomy. How do we understand the *greatness* of man as we saw in the last session—man made in God's image—and the *cruelty* and the *violence* of man that we see after the Fall? Has man lost everything that made him great? And the answer is *no*, he hasn't. But the image has been wrecked, and man has wrecked it by his own disobedience.

As we've already mentioned—and Bill made this point as well—that Adam and Eve were not affected by sin in the way that we are when it came time for them to evaluate Satan's proposition and to decide whether to believe God or to believe the Serpent. How much harder is it for us as fallen creatures? And I wouldn't disagree with your assessment about pridefulness. I think it was pridefulness that brought the first Fall in heaven. That Satan was not content to keep his proper place, rebelled against God, was cast out of heaven with the fallen angels, landed in the Garden, and then that cycle of pridefulness started all over again and continues to plague mankind. I sometimes see bumper stickers that say "The Power of Pride" and I think, yep, you have no idea—because it was pride that brought the first rebellion and just about every rebellion since.

From Perfection to Ruin

Now let's think about what this Fall was. I'm going to go back and reread the text one more time just so we can have it in the front of our minds as we consider this question. Starting at the beginning of chapter 3.

> Now the serpent was more crafty than any other beast of the field that the LORD God had made.

> He said to the woman, "Did God actually say, 'You shall not eat of any tree in the garden'?" And the woman said to the serpent, "We may eat of the fruit of the trees in the garden, but God said, 'You shall not eat of the fruit of the tree that is in the midst of the garden, neither shall you touch it, lest you die.'" But the serpent said to the woman, "You will not surely die. For God knows that when you eat of it your eyes will be opened, and you will be like God, knowing good and evil." So when the woman saw that the tree was good for food, and that it was a delight to the eyes, and that the tree was to be desired to make one wise, she took of its fruit and ate, and she also gave some to her husband who was with her, and he ate. Then the eyes of both were opened, and they knew that they were naked. And they sewed fig leaves together and made themselves loincloths.[51]

Now someone might raise the objection that this was a relatively small transgression. *What's the big deal about a bite of fruit?* And the answer is, *it's not a big deal.* The big deal is that that fruit is what God said you can't have. So it wasn't a question of how much they picked or how much they ate. It was a question of them taking it and eating it at all. Because that fruit represented—as we said in the last session—a boundary that God had placed around man's authority. God places Adam in the midst of the Garden and says, *all of these trees you can freely eat, but there's one that you can't eat.* It's as if God were saying, *that tree belongs to me, you leave that one alone.* And I don't think that's a far-fetched way to put it, because we can think, for example, when the first

---

[51] Gen 3:1-7 (ESV).

city in Canaan was conquered by the Israelites, what are we told about the things in that city, Jericho? That *the entire city was devoted to destruction.* That it was, as it were, an offering to the Lord, and none of what was found in the city was to be taken, and yet someone took one of the forbidden things. And it not only brought judgment against him and his household, but it indeed *brought judgment against the entire nation* that he had done that.

No Small Failure

So taking those things that God has said, *those belong to me*, is not a small matter. And so it's not really a question of the fruit *per se*, or what kind of fruit it was. It seems to be part of mythology that it was an apple, but the scripture doesn't tell us what kind of fruit it was. So it could have been any kind of fruit, and that didn't matter. What mattered was that God had set it apart for himself. And it also mattered what that fruit represented, not only the boundaries of *authority* of man, but also the boundaries of his *knowledge*, as we said last time. God does not intend for man to have knowledge of those things that God has hidden for himself. And so the severity of the transgression is that man was grasping for something that belonged exclusively to God—a portion of the creation that God has set aside outside of man's authority and the knowledge that it also represented.

Let me point your attention to the small book of Jude near the back of the Bible, right before the book of Revelation. There's an interesting allusion in the book of Jude about what happened in heaven. I'm going to start reading in verse six.

> And the angels who did not stay within their own position of authority, but left their proper dwelling, he has kept in eternal chains under gloomy darkness until the judgment of the great day—just as Sodom and Gomorrah and the surrounding cities, which likewise indulged in sexual immorality and pursued unnatural desire, serve as an example by undergoing a punishment of eternal fire.[52]

So what was the transgression of the angels? They were created perfect and glorious beings and set in heaven and given authority, but their transgression was an unwillingness to remain within the bounds of authority that God gave them. And when they left those proper bounds, they made themselves enemies of the one who set the boundaries. And the result that we read in the rest of that verse is sobering to say the least. What happens when you transgress the boundaries that God sets? *You place yourself under the judgment of God.* So it is no small matter. And that's quite like what has happened here in the Garden now. Adam and Eve have left the bounds of their authority. They've grasped for what was not theirs to grasp. They have said to themselves, *we are*

---

[52] Jude 6-7 (ESV).

not content with what God has provided for us. We're not content with the dominion that he's given us. We want something more. And so that brings about a catastrophic Fall. So the point of emphasis there is that, while we might trivialize this as a storybook kind of event—Adam and Eve taking an apple from the forbidden tree—it's far more than that, and we need to see it for what it is.

Trust or Doubt

If anyone has ever wondered if it seems reasonable that God should bring such a punishment upon Adam and Eve and upon the whole human race for such a seemingly small transgression, it's because we've not understood that it was not a small transgression at all. Again, to use the words of R.C. Sproul, he calls this *cosmic treason*. It's rebellion against the Creator. God sets the bounds, he gives every good thing, and then man oversteps the bounds.

This is the dilemma that we're all faced with. These are the two options that we have. When confronted with God's word, we basically have two choices. We can either *trust* what God's word says, or we can begin to *doubt* what God's word says. And when we begin to doubt, we are placing ourselves in judgment over the word of God. We are repeating the old question that the Serpent posed in the Garden, *has God said?*

And we are determining truth on the basis of our own senses, our own reason. We might say that the Enlightenment started in the Garden of Eden—attempting to evaluate truth on the basis of reason that has been divorced from the standard of the word of God.

The Bad News About Man's Condition

Now the bad news about man's condition is indeed bad. We saw just a glimpse of it by looking at a couple of verses at the beginning of Genesis 6. We'll look at a number of others just a bit later. But let's start by observing that man's condition is affected in his *mind*, in his *body*, and his *spirit*.[53] Death came into the world through sin. What does the scientist say about death? It's just a natural part of life. And yet anyone who's confronted with death, anyone who has had death visit his household, friends, family, siblings perhaps—you know that death is not a natural thing. You cannot look at someone whose life has left them and say that this is a natural thing. Morticians may do a good job of dressing up a corpse, but it's a corpse. The life is gone. And you can see that there is something *unnatural* about that. This was not part of God's original intent. We might forget that when God created Adam and Eve and placed them in the Garden, that they would have lived forever if

---

[53] I am not intending to suggest that man has a "three part" nature but that such descriptions as *body-soul-spirit* in 1 Thessalonians 5:23 are intended to describe man in his totality.

not for sin. Death was the intrusion. And the idea that death is somehow the mechanism for evolution does not fit the narrative at all.

So we have the death of the body. There is the aging and the decay process, disease, sometimes injury, so that we can now say that everyone dies. But not only that, there is what we call *spiritual* death as well. And one way we can think about spiritual death is that it's the loss of the ability to understand spiritual things. When we talked about the effects of idols earlier, when you're placing your trust in idols, when you become senseless, you cannot *think*, you cannot *see*, you cannot *hear*. These are the symptoms of spiritual death.

The mind is wrecked as well. If you haven't noticed, man has a remarkable ability in his fallen condition to rationalize what he wants to do. In fact, we see this happening even before the Fall. Isn't this exactly what Eve is doing? Look at verse 6 again in chapter 3:

> So when the woman saw that the tree was good for food, and that it was a delight to the eyes, and that the tree was to be desired to make one wise. . . .[54]

Classic rationalization. We can always find a justification for the sin that we want to engage in. And that is one of the characteristics,

---

[54] Gen 3:6 (ESV).

especially, of our fallen nature. We have a remarkable ability to justify all kinds of evil, individually and collectively.

Let's take a look at Romans 1:21. I want you to notice two things that it's describing in this verse. Paul says that

> . . . although they knew God . . .

—and we just saw that passage where Paul is saying that there is no one who has an excuse because God reveals Himself through the creation—

> For although they knew God, they did not honor him as God or give thanks to him, but they became futile in their thinking, and their foolish hearts were darkened.[55]

And there we see the *mind* and the *moral nature* being corrupted by sin. We cannot think properly.

And I'd also like to look at 1 Corinthians 2:14, which, referring to the spiritual nature, says that

> The natural person [the one who is not yet regenerate] does not accept the things of the Spirit of God, for they are folly to

---

[55] Rom 1:21 (ESV).

him, and he is not able to understand them because they are spiritually discerned.[56]

Spiritual discernment comes through spiritual wisdom. And where the Spirit of God is not, wisdom is not going to be there, either.

From Eden to Utopia

So we're beginning to get a picture of just how bad the Fall is. It's going to get worse, trust me. I'm not done yet. In the next item there in our notes I refer to *From Eden to Utopia*. And here's where I'm being a little sarcastic. Eden was a real place. Eden was, as scripture says, the *Paradise of God*, when God finished the creation of the heavens and the earth and placed the man and the woman in the Garden, it was a place of perfection. There was nothing lacking. As a footnote, I could add that I think part of the disadvantage of living on this side of the Fall is we don't realize how good it was at the beginning. Even on this side of the Flood, because I'm one of those who think that the world has drastically changed since the Flood. So you had the Fall that brought the original corruption, the loss of Paradise, and then the Flood that came about 1600 years later and completely reshaped the surface of the earth—so that the way things are today is nothing like what they were before. I think about how Noah lived for 350 years after the Flood. He was a very

---

[56] 1 Cor 2:14 (ESV).

important bridge from the antediluvian world to the world as we know it today, and what it must have been like for him to have lived for 600 years in that world *before* the Flood, and then to see how drastically it had been reshaped and reformed *afterward*.

But an even greater distortion is the one that comes from the Fall itself. We lost Eden in the Fall, and what have we been trying to do ever since because of this folly, that we said at the very beginning, that man thinks that he's basically good? If man is basically good, then certainly by a little bit of clever human effort, he is able to create Utopia. And yet the funny thing is, when I did a little word study on *utopia*—once again suspecting that it might be Greek—I found out, yes, it is. The root is *topos*. And I suspect that's the same word that we use for words like *topography*, referring to places. And the prefix (*ou-*) is a negation. So the Dickens translation of *utopia* is *a place that doesn't exist*. It's *noplace*. And yet it's that place that we're trying to create, having lost Eden by our disobedience, and now we are completely unable to recreate what was lost. It is beyond our power after the Fall to recreate Eden as Utopia.

When we were studying Genesis a few years ago, one of the patterns that we saw a number of times—and it begins here with the expulsion from the Garden—is that the man and the woman are driven out of the Garden to the *east*. And there's this idea that recurs throughout Genesis of going *east* and going *down*. And here, because I've watched way too many movies, I'm thinking of *Smokey and the Bandit*, where Jerry Reed sings the song, "Eastbound and Down." And that's the idea—that when you see man going eastward, like into the plain of Shinar, or when Lot goes eastward and down into the valley towards Sodom and Gomorrah, we're seeing a *decline*. And that's a fitting way to see what's happening here—that this is man grasping for something that he can't lay hold of. There is no Utopia.

Spiritual Warfare

Now, because this is a Fall that affects the spirit, we shouldn't be surprised that there is, as a result of this Fall, spiritual *warfare*. Where's the beginning of spiritual warfare? Where does that first show up? Well, here again, we say that this is one of those Christian doctrines that comes to us for the first time in the book of Genesis. After the Fall—we didn't read this passage, so let's take a look at it now. This is the Curse, God pronouncing the Curse, starting with the Serpent in verse 14:

> The LORD God said to the serpent,
>
> "Because you have done this,
>   cursed are you above all livestock
>   and above all beasts of the field;

> on your belly you shall go,
>   and dust you shall eat
>   all the days of your life.
> I will put enmity between you and the woman,
>   and between your offspring and her offspring;
> he shall bruise your head,
>   and you shall bruise his heel."[57]

Now if you look at surveys like Barna's surveys, they go out and ask people, and especially Christians, about different things. And you ask, *are we engaged in spiritual warfare?* The majority don't seem to think so. Most people seem not even to know that we are engaged in spiritual warfare, and yet that spiritual warfare started in the Garden. It started when Adam and Eve made themselves enemies of God, and it continues until the end of the age. And where else do we see that—the struggle, not just between flesh and blood, but as Paul would say, between *powers and principalities*? Ephesians 6, verse 12:

> For we do not wrestle against flesh and blood, but against the rulers, against the authorities, against the cosmic powers over this present darkness, against the spiritual forces of evil in the heavenly places.[58]

This is the spiritual battle. And we might even say that it requires some spiritual discernment just to realize that we are engaged in a spiritual

---

[57] Gen 3:14-15 (ESV).
[58] Eph 6:12 (ESV).

battle. And it's one of the reasons why we so desperately need scripture to help us discern the skirmishes in this spiritual battle so that we don't fall even further into temptation.

The Enemy's Tactics

Now let me suggest to you a few of the enemy's tactics These show up early on. And once again, it's kind of an accident that I alliterated these. But these all start with *D*.

Distortion.

Deception.

Distraction.

Denial.

And it's frankly alarming if you think about the tools that the enemy has at his disposal at the present day for all of those kinds of things. We've already said that we live in a culture that has denied objective truth and reason. So truth is gone. And what truth is there, is *distorted*. And then let's talk about *distraction*. Do we not live in an age of distraction, where everything is vying for our attention, even those things that you carry in your pocket all the time, always drawing your attention away from something else?

And we might say that Genesis 6 is bad enough in its evaluation, but I would hate to leave you there with the wrong impression that maybe it's not as bad as you think. Because it is. And it's important for us, and in the Reformed world, we call this the *depravity* of man. And we make such a big point of it in part because of how it affects our understanding of salvation. Because very simply, if you're not yet convinced that man, as Genesis would say, is *all bad all the time*, then you might be inclined to think that there is some small thing, some little good thing that you might contribute to your own salvation. And that's simply not possible given the condition of man's fallenness.

How Bad is Bad?

I'm going to start in Romans 1:28, and this is one of several passages that we might call *the litanies of sin*. Look at verse 28 to the end of chapter 1 in Romans.

> And since they did not see fit to acknowledge God, God gave them up to a debased mind to do what ought not to be done. They were filled with all manner of unrighteousness,

> evil, covetousness, malice. They are full of envy, murder, strife, deceit, maliciousness. They are gossips, slanderers, haters of God, insolent, haughty, boastful, inventors of evil, disobedient to parents, foolish, faithless, heartless, ruthless. Though they know God's righteous decree that those who practice such things deserve to die, they not only do them but give approval to those who practice them.[59]

And you might say, *well, thank goodness that that doesn't apply to us*. But then there's chapter 3, starting in verse 9. He's speaking to Jews here, but it applies to those who are part of this covenant.

> What then? Are we Jews any better off? No, not at all. For we have already charged that all, both Jews and Greeks, are under sin, as it is written:

And here he begins to quote from other parts of scripture. Paul does that a lot, by the way.

> "None is righteous, no, not one;
>   no one understands;
>   no one seeks for God.
> All have turned aside; together they have become worthless;
>   no one does good,
>   not even one."
> "Their throat is an open grave;
>   they use their tongues to deceive."
> "The venom of asps is under their lips."
>   "Their mouth is full of curses and bitterness."

---

[59] Rom 1:28-31 (ESV).

> "Their feet are swift to shed blood;
> > in their paths are ruin and misery,
> and the way of peace they have not known."
> > "There is no fear of God before their eyes."

That is the judgment against all mankind. He goes on to say:

> Now we know that whatever the law says it speaks to those who are under the law, so that every mouth may be stopped, and *the whole world may be held accountable to God.*

And then this is a verse that needs to settle into your heart and mind:

> For *by works of the law no human being will be justified in his sight,* since through the law comes knowledge of sin.[60]

It is the law that reveals to us what God requires. And if you say, like the rich young ruler, *yeah, yeah, I've done all that,* then you should hear the words of Jesus when he says, *be perfect just as your heavenly Father is perfect.* That's the standard. Why is it that if Adam and Eve had done everything right except taken one bite of the fruit, that it would have been enough to condemn the whole human race? And the answer is because it only takes one. Perfection is the standard and we're nowhere close to it.

---

[60] Rom 3:9-20 (ESV).

A couple of other passages. Let's go forward to the book of Galatians in chapter 5, starting in verse 19:

> Now the works of the flesh are evident: sexual immorality, impurity, sensuality, idolatry, sorcery, enmity, strife, jealousy, fits of anger, rivalries, dissensions, divisions, envy, drunkenness, orgies, and things like these. I warn you, as I warned you before, that those who do such things will not inherit the kingdom of God.[61]

And then turn over to Colossians chapter 3. Here Paul says starting in verse 5:

> Put to death therefore what is earthly in you: sexual immorality, impurity, passion, evil desire, and covetousness, which is idolatry. On account of these the wrath of God is coming. In these you too once walked, when you were living in them. But now you must put them all away: anger, wrath, malice, slander, and obscene talk from your mouth. Do not lie to one another, seeing that you have put off the old self with its practices and have put on the new self, which is being renewed in knowledge after the image of its creator.[62]

And so we see not only the sin that condemns, but we also see the renewal that comes through faith in Christ and the sanctification by the

---

[61] Gal 5:19-21 (ESV).
[62] Col 3:5-10 (ESV).

Word. What is it that we're being renewed into the likeness of? And that is the Lord himself.

I would also point your attention to Psalm 51:5. It's probably a familiar verse as well, where David says:

> Behold, I was brought forth in iniquity,
>   and in sin did my mother conceive me.[63]

Sin is that defect that is passed from generation to generation. There is no one who escapes it. There is only one whose conception was perfect and sinless—and that was Christ by the Holy Spirit. Everyone else from Cain onward has been conceived in sin and we don't have to look very hard in the birth and the life of Cain to see how sin—the sin of *Adam*—has been passed on to the next generation. And so it goes. The indictment is pretty severe. That's what we call the bad news. The good news is found in the gospel, which says that it's not by your effort that you can be saved.

I want you to notice a couple of things that are patterns that jump out at me when I look at Genesis 3 and 4. In Genesis chapter 3, after the Fall, we see that Adam and Eve sewed fig leaves together and made themselves loincloths. And these proved to be quite insufficient as

---

[63] Ps 51:5 (ESV).

covering for the guilt and the shame of their sin. God provided them a different covering a short time afterward, didn't he? Verse 21:

> And the LORD God made for Adam and for his wife *garments of skins* and clothed them.[64]

And there's the first indication that there has to be an innocent substitute. That we cannot stand in our own righteousness because we have none, but if God is to see us as righteous, we have to be clothed in the skins of a substitute. And we'll see this a bit more in the next session. But not only this. We have the contrast, as I would put it, between the *vegetables* that Adam and Eve tried to cover themselves with, and the *animals* that God covered them with. And then what do we see in the very next chapter when Cain and Abel bring their offerings to the Lord? One is acceptable and the other one isn't. Cain brings an offering of *vegetables* and Abel brings an offering from the *flock*. And so from very early on we begin to see that the proper worship of God is that there must be an offering for sin. There must be a substitute.

---

[64] Gen 3:21 (ESV).

"Who Then Can Be Saved?"

Well, if we understand just how severe man's condition is, and how truly helpless we are in regard to saving ourselves, the time for being saved by works has long since passed. Adam had that opportunity if he had obeyed the law of God—to bring salvation by works—but that's gone and it's lost. Now the question is, in our ruined condition—and this is one of those questions that's a really good question—*who then can be saved?*

Let's take a look at Luke 18. If the severity of the Fall is such that man can no longer save himself, then what is it going to take? This will be a familiar story. The rich young ruler comes to the Lord and questions Him.

> And a ruler asked him, "Good Teacher, what must I do to inherit eternal life?" And Jesus said to him, "Why do you call me good? No one is good except God alone."

Now let me stop there. What is the standard for righteousness? It's *divine*. Already we have the sense that this rich young ruler might want to be equivocating a little bit on the law, lowering the bar just a little bit so that he'll be able to say that he's met it. Jesus is already challenging that idea.

> "You know the commandments: 'Do not commit adultery, Do not murder, Do not steal, Do not bear false witness, Honor your father and mother.'" And he said, "All these I have kept from my youth."

Well, there's already a problem, isn't there? Because he hasn't kept *any* of those things. But he doesn't yet have the understanding of what God's law requires.

But Jesus plays along with this:

> When Jesus heard this, he said to him, "One thing you still lack."

A little sarcasm, *just one thing*.

> "Sell all that you have and distribute to the poor, and you will have treasure in heaven; and come, follow me." But when he heard these things, he became very sad, for he was extremely rich. Jesus, seeing that he had become sad, said, "How difficult it is for those who have wealth to enter the kingdom of God! For it is easier for a camel to go through the eye of a needle than for a rich person to enter the kingdom of God." Those who heard it said, "Then who can be saved?" But he said, "What is impossible with man is possible with God."[65]

---

[65] Luke 18:18-27 (ESV).

And God has made salvation possible not through your *works*, not through your *self-righteousness*, but through the person and the work of Christ who perfectly kept the law and who died an atoning death to satisfy the wrath of God for all your sin so that you can be heirs of eternal life with him in heaven forever.

Spurgeon says this:

> Everything that is evil lurks within the heart of every person. Education may restrain it, imitation of a good example may have some power in holding the monster down—but the very best of us, apart from the grace of God, placed under certain circumstances which would cause the evil within us to be developed rather than restrained—would soon prove to a demonstration that our nature was evil, and only evil, and that continually.

Amen.

Session 6: Redemption and Restoration

<u>Scripture (Gen 3:8-21)</u>

And they heard the sound of the Lord God walking in the garden in the cool of the day, and the man and his wife hid themselves from the presence of the Lord God among the trees of the garden. But the Lord God called to the man and said to him, "Where are you?" And he said, "I heard the sound of you in the garden, and I was afraid, because I was naked, and I hid myself." He said, "Who told you that you were naked? Have you eaten of the tree of which I commanded you not to eat?" The man said, "The woman whom you gave to be with me, she gave me fruit of the tree, and I ate." Then the Lord God said to the woman, "What is this that you have done?" The woman said, "The serpent deceived me, and I ate."

The Lord God said to the serpent,

> "Because you have done this,
>   cursed are you above all livestock
>   and above all beasts of the field;
> on your belly you shall go,
>   and dust you shall eat
>   all the days of your life.
> I will put enmity between you and the woman,
>   and between your offspring and her offspring;
> he shall bruise your head,
>   and you shall bruise his heel."

To the woman he said,

> "I will surely multiply your pain in childbearing;
>   in pain you shall bring forth children.

> Your desire shall be contrary to your husband,
>> but he shall rule over you."
>
> And to Adam he said,
>
>> "Because you have listened to the voice of your wife
>>> and have eaten of the tree
>> of which I commanded you,
>>> 'You shall not eat of it,'
>> cursed is the ground because of you;
>>> in pain you shall eat of it all the days of your life;
>> thorns and thistles it shall bring forth for you;
>>> and you shall eat the plants of the field.
>> By the sweat of your face
>>> you shall eat bread,
>> till you return to the ground,
>>> for out of it you were taken;
>> for you are dust,
>>> and to dust you shall return."
>
> The man called his wife's name Eve, because she was the mother of all living. And the Lord God made for Adam and for his wife garments of skins and clothed them.[66]

Introduction

I mentioned at the beginning of the last session that it's a very persistent myth among mankind, and going back as far as you want to go, that man is basically good. I did briefly come across something in a commentary about Genesis that made reference to the fact that in the

---

[66] Gen 3:8-21 (ESV).

histories of the ancient civilizations, even they were not willing to admit that there's something wrong with man. It's as if that, throughout history, the reality of the Fall and the effects of the Fall have been as thoroughly suppressed and scrubbed as we can make it. And so it's fitting that at the very beginning of Genesis, as God begins to record his Word in writing, that he tells us about this Fall, as if to make sure that it's not forgotten and lost.

Now, as it regards the state of man, the surveys tell us that man is basically good. And you might naturally expect that if you were to ask the next logical question, *how is it that we get to heaven?* The answer is, *by our good works.* And who's going to heaven? Well, of course *I* am. And why are you going to heaven? Because I think I've done more good than bad in my life—and that God is going to look at me and say, you did well enough, come on in.

But after what we discussed in the last section, it ought to be the case that we couldn't abide that idea, that God doesn't put our good and our bad works in a balance, so to speak, and say, well, as long as it tips just slightly in the direction of something that's good, then man has earned his salvation. The problem is actually pretty severe. If you were tracking with what we were describing in the last session, you would understand if I asked, *if we put our works in the balance, how would it work out?* And the answer is that all of our works would be on only one side of the scale, and that's all bad. There's nothing on the good side of the scale. Literally nothing. And you might say, well, *I'm really trying. I'm doing all these things. I'm serving God,* and so forth. But the problem is, as soon as you scratch the surface, you begin to discover that the reason that you're serving God is so that you can try to please him—that you think that by your works you can please him.

And I always find this rule to be the case in my own instance, that as soon as I realize how humble I am, I discover that there's a little bit of pride just underneath the surface. And that's our problem. That because of the fallenness, because of the effects of the Fall, because of the effects of the Curse, we really are utterly disabled and unable to do any good works. But there's nothing more American, I suppose, than thinking that you're basically good, that man is basically good, and that, of course, because you're basically good, of course, you're going to go to heaven. And that's a terrible deception. That is one of the Serpent's lies—that you are saved by your good works.

As we said last time, we ought to have this verse in our mind in Matthew 5, verse 48, where Jesus says, *be perfect even as your heavenly Father is perfect.* That's the standard. And you might say, well, I wasn't quite perfect yesterday. And then the response is, well, then it's too late.

You can't be saved by your works if you admit even a slight imperfection.

The High Price of a Soul

Now, when we look at how scripture describes salvation, there are different ways that it refers to it. And one of the words that we often use, and we may not think of it in its original usage, but we use the word *redemption*. What do we mean by that? Anybody in here use coupons? You *redeem* coupons or *redeem* credits or something of that sort? It's a monetary idea. It's a monetary transaction. And in fact, in more than one place, scripture refers to the Lord as the *Redeemer*. What does that mean? The question is, if man has lost his ability to gain heaven by his works, then what is it going to take? What is going to be the *price* that's necessary to get him into heaven? And there's a verse in Psalm 49 that I'd like you to consider. In verses 7-9 we read:

> Truly no man can ransom another,
>   or give to God the price of his life,
> for the ransom of their life is costly
>   and can never suffice,
> that he should live on forever
>   and never see the pit.[67]

---

[67] Ps 49:7-9 (ESV).

Now it seems pretty clear that what we're talking about is the ransom that's going to keep you out of the judgment of God. And what can one man pay on another man's behalf to turn aside, to get that person out of jail, so to speak? And the answer is, there's nothing that you can pay. The price is too high for one man to try to ransom the soul of the other. So we have this dilemma. Not only we can't save ourselves, but we cannot turn to the efforts of someone else to save us. We can't ask, as it were, for a letter of referral from our friend or maybe our pastor to get us into heaven. So we're left with this dilemma: how is the rebel—who has now fallen and who is under the effects of the Curse—going to be reconciled to his Creator? Is it even possible?

Not by the Works of the Law . . .

What we just read a short time ago in the story of the rich young ruler. The rich young ruler wasn't rich *enough* to get himself into heaven. He was rich enough to love his riches and be unwilling to let go of them. He might have had just a little bit of covetousness that needed to be dealt with, a little bit of idolatry. But his riches weren't going to get him into heaven. We saw also the story of the rich man and Lazarus. The rich man thought he was doing pretty well, but it didn't go well for him after his death.

How are we to be reconciled? Well, let's start with the *negative*. And here I'll point you back to Romans 3:20. We read this verse just a few moments ago. It bears repeating, where Paul says, after going through this litany of sins, the judgment against the fallenness of man, Jew and Gentile both being condemned in their sins:

> For *by works of the law no human being will be justified in his sight, since through the law comes knowledge of sin.*[68]

It's not going to happen by the works of the law. And where we see that human effort—just a moment ago, we were looking at the fact that after the Fall, Adam and Eve realized what? They were *naked* and they were *ashamed*. They were *guilty*. And they attempted to cover their guilt with fig leaves. And the fig leaves proved entirely inadequate to cover their guilt. It was not sufficient.

So we come to this conclusion that the opportunity to be saved by works is lost. But God in his gracious plan of salvation has made it possible for us to be saved by grace, through faith in Christ.

---

[68] Rom 3:20 (ESV).

. . . But by the Works of Another

So we have to turn to the works of another, the innocent substitute, as Mark just read there at the end of Genesis chapter 3, that *the Lord God made for Adam and for his wife garments of skins and clothed them.* Or as I would say it, *there was death in the Garden.* The death that Adam and Eve deserved was turned aside from them and directed at a substitute. In this case, an animal. We're not told it was a sheep, but we might suspect that it was.

We also see back in verse 15, in terms of the promise, looking at the strife that now exists between the seed of the Serpent and the Seed of the woman, that the day will come when the Seed of the woman will crush the head of the Serpent. So there is this promise of a victorious event. And we begin to see the picture of it at the end of this chapter when God makes skins for Adam and Eve. It's certainly not the fulfillment yet.

We might add to that what we read at the beginning of Hebrews, chapter 10, which is that *the blood of bulls and goats cannot take away sin.* So what then? Hebrews 10, verse 4:

> For it is impossible for the blood of bulls and goats to take away sins.[69]

We have these sacrifices. What was the point of the sacrificial system that began in the Garden—that was followed as we see in the very next chapter by Abel who offered a sacrifice that was acceptable to God and continued on. It was more formally instituted, we might say, in the Law of Moses several *thousand* years later with that sacrificial system. What's the point of that bloody system if all those sacrifices don't take away sin? They must be pointing to something, and by now it should be no surprise to say that these things are pointing forward to the one perfect sacrifice that will be accomplished by Christ on the cross. Here we are in the Garden—depending on whose chronology you like best, perhaps 4,500 B.C.—so several thousand years before Christ comes. But we already have the beginning of this redemption.

The Skins of the Elder Brother

There's another passage that I'd like to look at in the book of Genesis. It's one of those unseemly passages—not the worst of them—but it's not what you would call a great moment for our patriarchs. And that's found in Genesis chapter 27.

---

[69] Heb 10:4 (ESV).

Session 6: Redemption and Restoration

In Genesis chapter 27, we have Isaac blessing Jacob, but that's not quite what he intended to do, because he intended to bless Esau. But what did Rebekah and Jacob do? Hatched a little plan to make sure that Jacob would be the one who gets the blessing. Let me pick up the narrative in verse 18:

> So he went in to his father and said, "My father." And he said, "Here I am. Who are you, my son?" Jacob said to his father, "I am Esau your firstborn. I have done as you told me; now sit up and eat of my game, that your soul may bless me." But Isaac said to his son, "How is it that you have found it so quickly, my son?" He answered,

—and this is blasphemy—

> "Because the LORD your God granted me success." Then Isaac said to Jacob, "Please come near, that I may feel you, my son, to know whether you are really my son Esau or not." So Jacob went near to Isaac his father, who felt him and said, "The voice is Jacob's voice, but the hands are the hands of Esau." And he did not recognize him, because his hands were hairy like his brother Esau's hands.

Because why? He'd been covered in skins.

> So he blessed him. He said, "Are you really my son Esau?" He answered, "I am." Then he said, "Bring it near to me, that I may eat of my son's game and bless you." So he brought it near to him, and he ate; and he brought him wine, and he

drank. Then his father Isaac said to him, "Come near and kiss me, my son." So he came near and kissed him. And Isaac smelled the smell of his garments and blessed him and said,

> "See, the smell of my son
> is as the smell of a field that the LORD has blessed!"[70]

Because why? *He's wearing his brother's clothes.* He's been clothed in skins to simulate the hairy skin of his brother. He's wearing his brother's clothes that has the smell of the fields on it. His father suspects that something's a little off here, but nevertheless, his father is convinced in the end that this really is Jacob and not Esau.

Now again, this is not what you would call a great example to follow, but it does illustrate an interesting idea that here is the younger brother *impersonating*, as it were, the older brother by taking his older brother's clothes upon himself so that his father will see not the *younger* son but the *older*. That does have a familiar ring to it. It's interesting that throughout the book of Genesis from chapter 2 onward, this idea of clothing has such significance over and over again. And it also becomes a picture of salvation. And this is a case here where, as it were, if we put on the skins of our elder brother, the skins of righteousness, that when the Father draws us near, that he sees his elder Son who perfectly

---

[70] Gen 27:18-27 (ESV)

performed all the works of the Law, rather than the sin and the shame that those skins are covering in ourselves.

Let's take a look at 1 Corinthians 15. We've heard this idea that Adam was the representative of the human race when he was made and placed in the Garden and given a law and he disobeyed. Somebody might say that *it's not fair that Adam sinned, and now I'm guilty of Adam's sin*. But the fallacy is thinking that any one of us would have done better. The idea of representation is not a strange idea, certainly not to Americans. We have what's called a representative form of government. We delegate certain people to represent us. So this is very much like that. And we have, you might say, the first representation, Adam, the first man, who didn't do so well in his representation, which then necessitates a second man. And we see an example of that in 1 Corinthians 15. Let's look at 45 through 49.

> Thus it is written, "The first man Adam became a living being"; the last Adam became a life-giving spirit. But it is not the spiritual that is first but the natural, and then the spiritual. The first man was from the earth, a man of dust; the second man is from heaven. As was the man of dust, so also are those who are of the dust, and as is the man of heaven, so also are those who are of heaven. Just as we have borne the image of the man of dust, we shall also bear the image of the man of heaven.[71]

---

[71] 1 Cor 15:45-49 (ESV).

Adam represented it at first, at the beginning, created in the perfect image of God, lost much of that by his Fall, and we now see Jesus coming as the *second man* or the *last man* to do what Adam failed to do the first time—and we might say far more, for paying the price for sin.

Take a look also at verses 21 and 22 in the same chapter. We read:

> For as by a man came death, by a man has come also the resurrection of the dead. For as in Adam all die, so also in Christ shall all be made alive.[72]

I might add a footnote here that as we see this contrast between the first man, Adam, and the last man, Christ, what begins to happen to our apologetic of Christianity if we say, *well, the first man Adam wasn't really a man, he was just a myth?* The whole narrative falls apart. Everything depends upon that. I might also point out something obvious like the genealogy that traces the genealogy of Jesus all the way back to Adam.

Where Justice and Mercy Meet

So we have these historical figures, the first man and the last man. Christ fulfills the Law. He perfectly obeys the Law. This is where we see

---

[72] 1 Cor 15:21-22 (ESV).

justice and mercy meeting. We see the *wrath* of God that's being poured out on Christ, absorbing the penalty for sin so that he can then turn around and have *mercy* on those who deserve judgment. When we begin to understand the import of the work of Christ, it's not just absurd, but it's foolish to think that we could add anything to it to improve it. It's an affront to God if he has provided all that's necessary for salvation, for us to say, *but whoa, whoa, whoa, let me do a little bit myself. I want to do just a little bit.* No, there's nothing to be done. It's all been done. Three of the greatest words in scripture are the three words, *it is finished*. When Christ died on the cross, the work of redemption was fully accomplished. There was nothing to add to it.

<u>The Wages of Sin . . . and the Gift of Grace</u>

Flip back to Romans chapter 6. Let's be sure that we are thinking clearly about the relationship between *gifts* and *wages*. Verses 20 to 23. Paul says:

> For when you were slaves of sin, you were free in regard to righteousness. But what fruit were you getting at that time from the things of which you are now ashamed? For the end of those things is death. But now that you have been set free from sin and have become slaves of God, the fruit you get leads to sanctification and its end, eternal life. For the wages of sin is

> death, but the free gift of God is eternal life in Christ Jesus our Lord.[73]

And that's a phrase that's probably familiar, *the wages of sin is death*. What does that mean? It's the answer to the question, *what do you earn by your works?* Wages are what you earn. And the only thing that we can earn for ourselves in our fallen condition is death. Salvation *has* to be a free gift because there's nothing that we can do to *earn* it, and there's nothing that we can *add* to it.

Look at a couple of other verses, Romans 4:4, just flip back a page or so.

> Now to the one who works, his wages are not counted as a gift but as his due.[74]

If you've earned your wages, then you get paid. But if it's a gift, it's not something you earned. It's not something that you can earn.

And then I'd also like to look at a portion of John 6, starting in verse 60. This is a critical turning point in the ministry of Jesus. A bunch of those who have been following him are about to walk away.

---

[73] Rom 6:20-23 (ESV).
[74] Rom 4:4 (ESV).

When many of his disciples heard it, they said, "This is a hard saying; who can listen to it?" But Jesus, knowing in himself that his disciples were grumbling about this, said to them, "Do you take offense at this? Then what if you were to see the Son of Man ascending to where he was before? It is the Spirit who gives life; the flesh is no help at all. The words that I have spoken to you are spirit and life. But there are some of you who do not believe." (For Jesus knew from the beginning who those were who did not believe, and who it was who would betray him.) And he said, "This is why I told you that no one can come to me unless it is granted him by the Father." After this many of his disciples turned back and no longer walked with him.[75]

Very clear teaching on the futility of works righteousness. We cannot earn our salvation. Jesus has taught through these first few chapters about the work of the Spirit. And here he says explicitly that *it is the Spirit who gives life, and that the flesh is nothing, is no profit.*

Recap: Hard Questions—*Answered*

So as we begin to close the loop on our study of Genesis today, let's go back to our original thinking. We said that one of the reasons for Genesis is that it helps us to answer the hard questions. It helps to bring clarity out of our confusion—especially in our fallenness. And has it done that? Are we beginning to see how it sets the foundation for our

---

[75] John 6:60-66 (ESV).

faith? We learned something about who God is. We learned something about who we are. We're beginning to learn what God has done for us. We begin to see how, in salvation, we're being renewed after the image of Christ—that what we lost in the Fall is to be regained and perfected. And that is the work of sanctification and glorification.

As we bring our study today to a conclusion, I would like one last time to go back to the book of Genesis, this time to chapter 22. I'm going to start at the beginning of the chapter and read the first 14 verses. This is the account of God calling Abraham to sacrifice his son Isaac.

> After these things God tested Abraham and said to him, "Abraham!" And he said, "Here I am." He said, "Take your son, your only son Isaac, whom you love, and go to the land of Moriah, and offer him there as a burnt offering on one of the mountains of which I shall tell you." So Abraham rose early in the morning, saddled his donkey, and took two of his young men with him, and his son Isaac. And he cut the wood for the burnt offering and arose and went to the place of which God had told him. On the third day Abraham lifted up his eyes and saw the place from afar. Then Abraham said to his young men, "Stay here with the donkey; I and the boy will go over there and worship and come again to you." And Abraham took the wood of the burnt offering and laid it on Isaac his son. And he took in his hand the fire and the knife. So they went both of them together. And Isaac said to his father Abraham, "My father!" And he said, "Here I am, my son." He said, "Behold, the fire and the wood, but where is the lamb for a burnt offering?" Abraham said, "God will provide for himself the

> lamb for a burnt offering, my son." So they went both of them together.
>
> When they came to the place of which God had told him, Abraham built the altar there and laid the wood in order and bound Isaac his son and laid him on the altar, on top of the wood. Then Abraham reached out his hand and took the knife to slaughter his son. But the angel of the LORD called to him from heaven and said, "Abraham, Abraham!" And he said, "Here I am." He said, "Do not lay your hand on the boy or do anything to him, for now I know that you fear God, seeing you have not withheld your son, your only son, from me." And Abraham lifted up his eyes and looked, and behold, behind him was a ram, caught in a thicket by his horns. And Abraham went and took the ram and offered it up as a burnt offering instead of his son. So Abraham called the name of that place, "The LORD will provide"; as it is said to this day, "On the mount of the LORD it shall be provided."[76]

And that name that God reveals Himself as, is *Jehovah-Jireh*. And I prefer the definite object in that expression, that the Lord will provide *it*. Not just that the Lord will *provide*, as if it's a general expression, but the Lord will provide *it*. Provide *what*? Provide the sacrifice, the substitute. You see, every one of us is Isaac on that bed of wood. Was this a case of God telling Abraham to murder his son? No. Murder comes from the heart. It comes from hatred. Abraham loved his son and would not have harmed him. But the test was *what*? To discover whether Abraham loved God more than he loved his son—and to

---

[76] Gen 22:1-14 (ESV)

realize that Isaac deserved to die for his own sin. And here is this picture in graphic form of God providing that substitute. It's the Lord Jesus who stands in the place of every sinner, taking the wrath of God. God putting his own beloved Son to death, so that sinners can be saved and redeemed.

Luther says this—and it wouldn't be much of a Reformation weekend if we didn't quote Martin Luther at least once:

> From the beginning of my Reformation, I have asked God to send me neither dreams, nor visions, nor angels, but to give me the right understanding of His Word, the Holy Scriptures; for as long as I have God's Word, I know that I am walking in His way, and that I shall not fall into any error or delusion.

Amen.

About J.R. Dickens

J.R. Dickens holds a Ph.D. in mechanical engineering and has frequently served as a lay teacher in the church over the course of more than twenty years. His most extensive teaching topics include the book of Genesis, biblical creation, apologetics, and the *Westminster Confession of Faith*.

J.R. is the author of the *Coffee Talk* series of short books on Christian apologetics, as well as a timely booklet on the importance of recovering ecclesiastical authority.

In the spring of 2023, J.R. was invited to teach *The Apologetics of Francis Schaeffer* at New Geneva Theological Seminary in Colorado Springs, Colorado, where he has also served as librarian for a collection of 25,000 printed titles.

J.R.'s personal interests include aviation, where he holds a commercial pilot certificate, instrument rating, and flight instructor rating. He also enjoys camping, hiking, and skiing.

J.R. can be reached by email at *jrdickens90@gmail.com*. His books are available on Amazon and many of his messages can be heard on SermonAudio.

www.ingramcontent.com/pod-product-compliance
Lightning Source LLC
LaVergne TN
LVHW051601070426
835507LV00021B/2702